A Gift for

....

From

....

Date

....

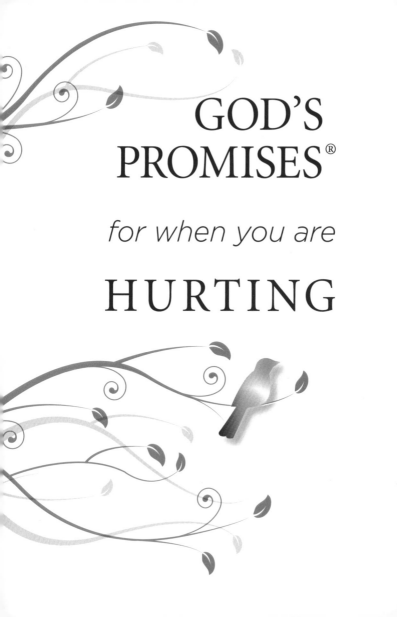

GOD'S
PROMISES®

for when you are

HURTING

GOD'S
PROMISES®

for when you are

HURTING

BY JACK COUNTRYMAN

A Division of Thomas Nelson Publishers

THOMAS NELSON
Since 1798

NASHVILLE   MEXICO CITY   RIO DE JANEIRO

ISBN-13: 978-0-7180-3417-7

Printed in China

16 17 18 TIMS 5 4 3

www.thomasnelson.com

TABLE OF CONTENTS

TRUTH FROM THE BIBLE ABOUT . . .

INTRODUCTION

So many times in life we are faced with challenges and disappointment. Thankfully, God has given us His encouraging words of Scripture for answers to life's difficult circumstances. This book has been designed to help you if you're hurting: God's promises and truths offer comfort and peace when life is hard. Our prayer is that, as a result of spending time in God's Word, you will experience His peace that passes all understanding.

TRUTH

for when you are feeling . . .

DISCOURAGED

Whenever God allows you to experience more demands, setbacks, and even pain than you think you can handle, it's easy to become overwhelmed and find yourself discouraged. Why even get up in the morning when the burdens are so heavy and the path ahead unclear? Because in seasons like these, you can experience the bittersweet closeness of your heavenly Father who will enable you—by His power and His presence—to stand strong in every trial and to navigate every tribulation. He has been faithful through the ages, He is faithful now, and He will be your strength whatever problems you face.

*Greatly rejoice, though now for a little while, if
need be, you have been grieved by various trials,
that the genuineness of your faith, being much
more precious than gold that perishes, though it
is tested by fire, may be found to praise, honor,
and glory at the revelation of Jesus Christ, whom
having not seen you love.*

1 PETER 1:6–8

*Though I walk in the midst of trouble, You will
     revive me;
You will stretch out Your hand
    Against the wrath of my enemies,
    And Your right hand will save me.
The LORD will perfect that which concerns me;
    Your mercy, O LORD, endures forever;
    Do not forsake the works of Your hands.*

PSALM 138:7–8

"I am with you always, even to the end of the age."

MATTHEW 28:20

"Let not your heart be troubled; you believe in God, believe also in Me. In My Father's house are many mansions; if it were not so, I would have told you. I go to prepare a place for you. And if I go and prepare a place for you, I will come again and receive you to Myself; that where I am, there you may be also."

JOHN 14:1–3

"Peace I leave with you, My peace I give to you; not as the world gives do I give to you. Let not your heart be troubled, neither let it be afraid."

JOHN 14:27

Let us run with endurance the race that is set before us, looking unto Jesus, the author and finisher of our faith.

HEBREWS 12:1–2

[Be] confident of this very thing, that He who has begun a good work in you will complete it until the day of Jesus Christ.

Philippians 1:6

Love the Lord, all you godly ones!
*   For the Lord protects those who are loyal to*
*   him,*
*   but he harshly punishes the arrogant.*
So be strong and courageous,
*   all you who put your hope in the Lord!*

Psalm 31:23–24 NLT

LONELY

Loneliness can weigh down your heart, erode your confidence, and rob you of hope. If that's where you are right now, consider this: Jesus Himself was lonely when, early in His ministry, His family didn't understand Him. Jesus was lonely when His disciples were slow to recognize Him and slow to understand why He had come. And Jesus undoubtedly felt very much alone when Judas betrayed Him and Peter denied knowing Him. Jesus understands your loneliness. Turn to Him who is with you throughout every day and every night, and you'll find in Him the sweetest companionship you'll ever know.

*Blessed be the God and Father of our Lord Jesus
Christ, the Father of mercies and God of all
comfort, who comforts us in all our tribulation.*

2 CORINTHIANS 1:3–4

*God is our refuge and strength,
    A very present help in trouble. . . .
The LORD of hosts is with us;
    The God of Jacob is our refuge.*

PSALM 46:1, 7

*I am persuaded that neither death nor life,
nor angels nor principalities nor powers, nor
things present nor things to come, nor height nor
depth, nor any other created thing, shall be able
to separate us from the love of God which is in
Christ Jesus our Lord.*

ROMANS 8:38–39

Draw near to God and He will draw near to you.

JAMES 4:8

The LORD your God, He is the One who goes
with you. He will not leave you nor forsake you.

DEUTERONOMY 31:6

"For the mountains shall depart
    And the hills be removed,
    But My kindness shall not depart from you,
    Nor shall My covenant of peace be removed,"
Says the LORD, who has mercy on you.

ISAIAH 54:10

There is no one like the God of Jeshurun,
    Who rides the heavens to help you,
    And in His excellency on the clouds.
The eternal God is your refuge,
    And underneath are the everlasting arms.

DEUTERONOMY 33:26–27

[The LORD] heals the brokenhearted
And binds up their wounds.
He counts the number of the stars;
He calls them all by name.
Great is our LORD, and mighty in power;
His understanding is infinite.

PSALM 147:3–5

DEPRESSED

Sometimes your world is gray. Dark gray. Sometimes you know why, but other times you don't. Whatever its source, that gray can weigh you down and deplete your energy and enthusiasm for life. It can cause you to isolate yourself, and it can make doubts grow to daunting proportions. But the truth in God's Word can shine light into the gray. So, however gray your world is right now, choose to believe God's promise that—even if you don't feel hope and even if you can't imagine how it could happen—He brings beauty out of ashes. Your almighty Savior does that because He dearly loves you. And because you are His and because He is God, no one can take away His love for you.

[The LORD's] favor is for life;
   Weeping may endure for a night,
   But joy comes in the morning.

PSALM 30:5

The Spirit of the Lord GOD is upon Me,
   Because the LORD has anointed Me . . .
   To heal the brokenhearted . . .
To console those who mourn in Zion,
   To give them beauty for ashes,
   The oil of joy for mourning,
   The garment of praise for the spirit of
      heaviness;
   That they may be called trees of
      righteousness,
   The planting of the LORD, that He may be
      glorified.

ISAIAH 61:1, 3

The eyes of the LORD *are on the righteous,*
    And His ears are open to their cry. . . .
The righteous cry out, and the LORD *hears,*
    And delivers them out of all their troubles.
The LORD *is near to those who have a*
       broken heart,
    And saves such as have a contrite spirit.

                               PSALM 34:15, 17–18

Blessed be the God and Father of our Lord Jesus
Christ, the Father of mercies and God of all
comfort, who comforts us in all our tribulation,
that we may be able to comfort those who are
in any trouble, with the comfort with which
we ourselves are comforted by God. For as
the sufferings of Christ abound in us, so our
consolation also abounds through Christ.

                            2 CORINTHIANS 1:3–5

When you pass through the waters, I will be
    with you;
    And through the rivers, they shall not
    overflow you. . . .
For I am the LORD your God,
    The Holy One of Israel, your Savior.

ISAIAH 43:2–3

[The LORD] gives power to the weak,
    And to those who have no might He increases
    strength.
Even the youths shall faint and be weary,
    And the young men shall utterly fall,
But those who wait on the LORD
    Shall renew their strength;
    They shall mount up with wings like eagles,
    They shall run and not be weary,
    They shall walk and not faint.

ISAIAH 40:29–31

WORRIED

Life in this fallen world can provide much to worry about. Add to that humankind's propensity to focus on all the what-ifs, your thoughts can actually fuel the fire of worry. Satan will use worry to cause doubts, confusion, and insecurity. He will also use your worries to keep you focused on circumstances rather than on God and His faithfulness. Freedom from worry can come when you choose to think about God's truth—however contrary to reality it seems—rather than on whatever is prompting you to worry. Focusing on God's Word and His power will replace your worry with peace. After all, you are a child of the King, and His truth is your shield.

You will keep him in perfect peace,
Whose mind is stayed on You,
Because he trusts in You.
Trust in the Lord *forever,*
For in YAH, the Lord, *is everlasting*
strength.

Isaiah 26:3–4

Be anxious for nothing, but in everything by prayer
and supplication, with thanksgiving, let your
requests be made known to God; and the peace of
God, which surpasses all understanding, will guard
your hearts and minds through Christ Jesus.

Philippians 4:6–7

Put on love, which is the bond of perfection. And
let the peace of God rule in your hearts, to which
also you were called in one body; and be thankful.

Colossians 3:14–15

My God shall supply all your need according to
His riches in glory by Christ Jesus.

PHILIPPIANS 4:19

Humble yourselves under the mighty hand of
God, that He may exalt you in due time, casting
all your care upon Him, for He cares for you.

1 PETER 5:6–7

"Do not worry, saying, 'What shall we eat?' or
'What shall we drink?' or 'What shall we wear?'
For after all these things the Gentiles seek. For
your heavenly Father knows that you need all
these things. But seek first the kingdom of God
and His righteousness, and all these things shall
be added to you. Therefore do not worry about
tomorrow, for tomorrow will worry about its own
things. Sufficient for the day is its own trouble."

MATTHEW 6:31–34

Those who live according to the flesh set their minds on the things of the flesh, but those who live according to the Spirit, the things of the Spirit. For to be carnally minded is death, but to be spiritually minded is life and peace.

ROMANS 8:5–6

He who dwells in the secret place of the
     Most High
     Shall abide under the shadow of the
     Almighty.
I will say of the LORD, *"He is my refuge and*
     my fortress;
     My God, in Him I will trust."
Surely He shall deliver you from the snare of
     the fowler
     And from the perilous pestilence.
He shall cover you with His feathers,
     And under His wings you shall take refuge;
     His truth shall be your shield and buckler.

PSALM 91:1–4

CONFUSED

In today's noisy world with its various voices calling you in different directions, it's easy to find yourself confused. The loud and contradictory messages the world speaks about your value and purpose, about what to believe and how to live, can definitely cause uncertainty about specific situations and about who you are in general. By God's grace, though, He has provided His Word of truth. You can open the pages of Scripture and find all the answers you need. So take time to get away from the noise and spend quiet time alone with Him, reading and believing His promises to you. He will direct your path toward peace, contentment, and clarity—gifts that only He can give.

*Trust in the L*ORD *with all your heart,*
    And lean not on your own understanding;
In all your ways acknowledge Him,
    And He shall direct your paths.

PROVERBS 3:5–6

The wisdom that is from above is first pure, then peaceable, gentle, willing to yield, full of mercy and good fruits, without partiality and without hypocrisy. Now the fruit of righteousness is sown in peace by those who make peace.

JAMES 3:17–18

*Cast your burden on the L*ORD,
    And He shall sustain you;
    He shall never permit the righteous to
        be moved.

PSALM 55:22

God has not given us a spirit of fear, but of power and of love and of a sound mind.

2 TIMOTHY 1: 7

"The Lord GOD will help Me;
    Therefore I will not be disgraced;
    Therefore I have set My face like a flint,
    And I know that I will not be ashamed.
He is near who justifies Me;
    Who will contend with Me?
    Let us stand together.
    Who is My adversary?
    Let him come near Me. . . .
"Who among you fears the LORD?
    Who obeys the voice of His Servant?
    Who walks in darkness
    And has no light?
    Let him trust in the name of the LORD
    And rely upon his God."

ISAIAH 50:7–8, 10

You are my hiding place;
    You shall preserve me from trouble;
    You shall surround me with songs of
        deliverance. Selah
I will instruct you and teach you in the way you
        should go;
    I will guide you with My eye.

PSALM 32:7–8

The LORD *will wait, that He may be gracious to*
        you;
    And therefore He will be exalted, that He
        may have mercy on you.
    For the LORD *is a God of justice;*
    Blessed are all those who wait for Him. . . .
Your ears shall hear a word behind you, saying,
    "This is the way, walk in it,"
    Whenever you turn to the right hand
    Or whenever you turn to the left."

ISAIAH 30:18, 21

FEARFUL

The Lord calls you to keep your eyes on Him throughout life's journey. He has promised to provide all that you need, including strength, wisdom, and guidance. But God's enemy and yours—Satan himself—will whisper in your ear to stir up fear instead of faith. Fear can shift your focus from God to self. Fear can draw you inward, distance you from the Lord, and deafen you to the leading of the Holy Spirit. Your heart and mind then become Satan's playground, and he causes you to doubt your relationship with your heavenly Father. God's truth, set forth in His Word, shines its bright light on the enemy's lies. Open its pages and let God's perfect love—evident from Genesis through Revelation—cast out all your fear.

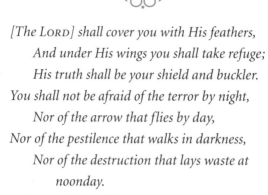

[The Lord] shall cover you with His feathers,
   And under His wings you shall take refuge;
   His truth shall be your shield and buckler.
You shall not be afraid of the terror by night,
   Nor of the arrow that flies by day,
Nor of the pestilence that walks in darkness,
   Nor of the destruction that lays waste at
      noonday.
A thousand may fall at your side,
   And ten thousand at your right hand;
   But it shall not come near you.

Psalm 91:4–7

Whatever things are true, whatever things are
noble, whatever things are just, whatever things
are pure, whatever things are lovely, whatever
things are of good report, if there is any virtue
and if there is anything praiseworthy—meditate
on these things.

Philippians 4:8

As many as are led by the Spirit of God, these are sons of God. For you did not receive the spirit of bondage again to fear, but you received the Spirit of adoption by whom we cry out, "Abba, Father." The Spirit Himself bears witness with our spirit that we are children of God, and if children, then heirs—heirs of God and joint heirs with Christ, if indeed we suffer with Him, that we may also be glorified together.

ROMANS 8:14–17

Because you have made the LORD, who is my refuge,
Even the Most High, your dwelling place,
No evil shall befall you,
Nor shall any plague come near your dwelling;
For He shall give His angels charge over you,
To keep you in all your ways.

PSALM 91:9–11

In righteousness you shall be established;
You shall be far from oppression, for you
shall not fear;
And from terror, for it shall not come near you.

ISAIAH 54:14

Yea, though I walk through the valley of the
shadow of death,
I will fear no evil;
For You are with me;
Your rod and Your staff, they comfort me.
You prepare a table before me in the presence of
my enemies;
You anoint my head with oil;
My cup runs over.

PSALM 23:4–5

AFRAID AND NEED COURAGE

At times you may be absolutely sure about what you need to do—but you're afraid. At other times you are confident that God is nudging you to speak certain words or make a specific decision—but you lack the courage to step out in faith. When you sense what God wants you to do but feel nervous about doing it, know that He will give you the courage you need. As you prayerfully take the first step, you'll experience God's strength. Your heavenly Father—the almighty God—will give you strength for every situation you face. When you rely on His power, you will be able to run and not be weary; you will be able to persevere and not be faint. That is God's promise to you.

"Fear not, for I am with you;
  Be not dismayed, for I am your God.
  I will strengthen you,
  Yes, I will help you,
  I will uphold you with My righteous right
    hand."

ISAIAH 41:10

Wait on the LORD;
  Be of good courage,
  And He shall strengthen your heart;
  Wait, I say, on the LORD!

PSALM 27:14

"Who gave human beings their mouths? Who makes them deaf or mute? Who gives them sight or makes them blind? Is it not I, the Lord? Now go; I will help you speak and will teach you what to say."

EXODUS 4:11–12 NIV

*I am persuaded that neither death nor life,
nor angels nor principalities nor powers, nor
things present nor things to come, nor height nor
depth, nor any other created thing, shall be able
to separate us from the love of God which is in
Christ Jesus our Lord.*

ROMANS 8:38–39

*[God] gives power to the weak,
    And to those who have no might He increases
        strength.
Even the youths shall faint and be weary,
    And the young men shall utterly fall,
But those who wait on the LORD
    Shall renew their strength;
    They shall mount up with wings like eagles,
    They shall run and not be weary,
    They shall walk and not faint.*

ISAIAH 40:29–31

*Thus says the L*ORD*, who created you, O Jacob,*
   And He who formed you, O Israel:
   "Fear not, for I have redeemed you;
   I have called you by your name;
   You are Mine.
When you pass through the waters, I will be
      with you;
   And through the rivers, they shall not
      overflow you.
   When you walk through the fire, you shall
      not be burned,
   Nor shall the flame scorch you.
*For I am the L*ORD *your God,*
   The Holy One of Israel, your Savior."

                              ISAIAH 43:1–3

Be of good courage,
   And He shall strengthen your heart,
   *All you who hope in the L*ORD*.*

                              PSALM 31:24

ANGRY

There is righteous anger—that fury you feel about what you know God disproves of. But too often anger is less noble. You feel angry, for instance, when you don't get your way, or the day isn't unfolding according to your timetable, or people let you down, or . . . The list goes on. Aware that much in this world can cause you to rage, God calls you to be "slow to wrath" (James 1:19). Don't let anger be your master, prompting you to say or do things you will later regret. Anger can fuel foolishness and even harm, but with God's help you can corral your anger before any damage is done. That option is always the best one.

Let every man be swift to hear, slow to speak, slow to wrath; for the wrath of man does not produce the righteousness of God.

JAMES 1:19–20

Putting away lying, "Let each one of you speak truth with his neighbor," for we are members of one another. "Be angry, and do not sin": do not let the sun go down on your wrath, nor give place to the devil.

EPHESIANS 4:25–27

A soft answer turns away wrath,
But a harsh word stirs up anger.
The tongue of the wise uses knowledge rightly,
But the mouth of fools pours forth foolishness.

PROVERBS 15:1–2

He who is slow to wrath has great understanding,
  But he who is impulsive exalts folly.

PROVERBS 14:29

He who is slow to anger is better than the mighty,
  And he who rules his spirit than he who
    takes a city.

PROVERBS 16:32

If your enemy is hungry, give him bread to eat;
  And if he is thirsty, give him water to drink;
For so you will heap coals of fire on his head,
  And the LORD will reward you.

PROVERBS 25:21–22

Let all bitterness, wrath, anger, clamor, and
evil speaking be put away from you, with
all malice. And be kind to one another,
tenderhearted, forgiving one another, even as
God in Christ forgave you.

EPHESIANS 4:31–32

Put off all these: anger, wrath, malice, blasphemy, filthy language out of your mouth. Do not lie to one another, since you have put off the old man with his deeds, and have put on the new man who is renewed in knowledge according to the image of Him who created him.

COLOSSIANS 3:8–10

Do not hasten in your spirit to be angry,
*   For anger rests in the bosom of fools.*

ECCLESIASTES 7:9

A wise man fears and departs from evil,
*   But a fool rages and is self-confident.*
A quick-tempered man acts foolishly,
*   And a man of wicked intentions is hated.*

PROVERBS 14:16–17

OVERCOME BY GRIEF

The pain of loss—especially of losing someone you dearly love—can be overwhelming and even incapacitating. Life can bring heartache more painful than you ever thought possible. In those times God can seem distant and even uncaring, but neither is true. God promises in His Word to be with you always, so whatever your feelings suggest, know that He is with you. He also promises to comfort you whenever you grieve a loss. He will carry you when you cannot put one foot in front of another, so receive and rest in His comforting presence with you.

*Blessed be the God and Father of our Lord Jesus
Christ, the Father of mercies and God of all
comfort, who comforts us in all our tribulation,
that we may be able to comfort those who are
in any trouble, with the comfort with which we
ourselves are comforted by God.*

2 CORINTHIANS 1:3–4

*[Since] we believe that Jesus died and rose again,
even so God will bring with Him those who sleep
in Jesus.*

1 THESSALONIANS 4:14

*Now may our Lord Jesus Christ Himself, and our
God and Father, who has loved us and given us
everlasting consolation and good hope by grace,
comfort your hearts and establish you in every
good word and work.*

2 THESSALONIANS 2:16–17

"Blessed are those who mourn,
    For they shall be comforted."

MATTHEW 5:4

"O Death, where is your sting?
    O Hades, where is your victory?"

1 CORINTHIANS 15:55

I heard a loud voice from heaven saying,
"Behold, the tabernacle of God is with men, and
He will dwell with them, and they shall be His
people. God Himself will be with them and be
their God. And God will wipe away every tear
from their eyes; there shall be no more death, nor
sorrow, nor crying. There shall be no more pain,
for the former things have passed away."

REVELATION 21:3–4

Remember the word to Your servant,
     Upon which You have caused me to hope.
This is my comfort in my affliction,
     For Your word has given me life.

PSALM 119:49–50

IMPATIENT

Do you tend to want everything immediately? It's hard not to in this microwave age, but few good things come quickly. Yet some people seem, by nature, to be more patient than others, but seasons of waiting can test even the most patient people you know. When answers to prayer don't come quickly, when God gives you an opportunity to persevere in difficult circumstances or a challenging relationship, or when the darkness of your life seems impenetrable, turn to the Savior. Ask Him to enable you to be patient. Remind yourself that He uses periods of waiting to grow your faith and refine your character. Choose to cling to the rock-solid fact that God is sovereign and His timing is perfect. And remember to breathe.

The Lord is good to those who wait for Him,
    To the soul who seeks Him.
It is good that one should hope and wait quietly
    For the salvation of the Lord.

LAMENTATIONS 3:25–26

Wait on the Lord;
    Be of good courage,
    And He shall strengthen your heart;
    Wait, I say, on the Lord!

PSALM 27:14

Do not become sluggish, but imitate those who
through faith and patience inherit the promises.

HEBREWS 6:12

*Hope that is seen is not hope; for why does one
still hope for what he sees? But if we hope for
what we do not see, we eagerly wait for it with
perseverance.*

ROMANS 8:24–25

*Whatever things were written before were
written for our learning, that we through the
patience and comfort of the Scriptures might
have hope. Now may the God of patience and
comfort grant you to be like-minded toward one
another, according to Christ Jesus.*

ROMANS 15:4–5

*I waited patiently for the LORD;
    And He inclined to me,
    And heard my cry. . . .
He has put a new song in my mouth—
    Praise to our God;
    Many will see it and fear,
    And will trust in the LORD.*

PSALM 40:1, 3

We also glory in tribulations, knowing that tribulation produces perseverance; and perseverance, character; and character, hope. Now hope does not disappoint, because the love of God has been poured out in our hearts by the Holy Spirit who was given to us.

ROMANS 5:3–5

RESTLESS

The realities of life can be unsettling. Responsibilities can weigh heavily. Trials and tribulations can bring uncertainty and even hopelessness. Seemingly impossible situations can be puzzling. Much in this world can try to rob you of peace. But you can prevent that robbery when you choose to trust in the Lord, when you decide to remember His faithfulness through the years, and when you focus on truths like His sovereignty, His unlimited power, and His unshakable love for you. Choose to trust in the Lord today, and embrace the lasting peace that only He can give.

*Be anxious for nothing, but in everything by
prayer and supplication, with thanksgiving, let
your requests be made known to God; and the
peace of God, which surpasses all understanding,
will guard your hearts and minds through Christ
Jesus.*

PHILIPPIANS 4:6–7

*"Peace I leave with you, My peace I give to you;
not as the world gives do I give to you. Let not
your heart be troubled, neither let it be afraid."*

JOHN 14:27

*Those who live according to the flesh set their
minds on the things of the flesh, but those who
live according to the Spirit, the things of the
Spirit. For to be carnally minded is death, but to
be spiritually minded is life and peace.*

ROMANS 8:5–6

*The kingdom of God is not eating and drinking,
but righteousness and peace and joy in the Holy
Spirit. For he who serves Christ in these things is
acceptable to God and approved by men.*

*Therefore let us pursue the things which
make for peace and the things by which one may
edify another.*

ROMANS 14:17–19

*Be of good comfort, be of one mind, live in peace;
and the God of love and peace will be with you.*

2 CORINTHIANS 13:11

*May the God of hope fill you with all joy and
peace in believing, that you may abound in hope
by the power of the Holy Spirit.*

ROMANS 15:13

*Great peace have those who love Your law,
And nothing causes them to stumble.*

PSALM 119:165

The righteous perishes,

> *And no man takes it to heart;*
> *Merciful men are taken away,*
> *While no one considers*
> *That the righteous is taken away from evil.*

He shall enter into peace;

> *They shall rest in their beds,*
> *Each one walking in his uprightness.*

Isaiah 57:1–2

DOUBTFUL ABOUT GOD'S GOODNESS

Strong evidence exists for Jesus' resurrection. Science supports creationism. Personal experiences can serve as compelling arguments for the reality of the supernatural. Your choice is to believe or not believe. When you're hurting, though, the choice to believe is tough: *Is God hearing my prayers? Will He meet my needs? Does He really care?* If you find yourself doubting, talk to God about your doubts (He's already aware of them!) and then open His Word. Read the words of Scripture and choose faith. Choose to believe.

Lord, I believe; help my unbelief!

MARK 9:24

"Have faith in God. For assuredly, I say to you, whoever says to this mountain, 'Be removed and be cast into the sea,' and does not doubt in his heart, but believes that those things he says will be done, he will have whatever he says. Therefore I say to you, whatever things you ask when you pray, believe that you receive them, and you will have them."

MARK 11:22–24

"Do not seek what you should eat or what you should drink, nor have an anxious mind. For all these things the nations of the world seek after, and your Father knows that you need these things. But seek the kingdom of God, and all these things shall be added to you."

LUKE 12:29–31

[Abraham] did not waver at the promise of God through unbelief, but was strengthened in faith, giving glory to God, and being fully convinced that what He had promised He was also able to perform.

ROMANS 4:20–21

The Lord is not slack concerning His promise, as some count slackness, but is longsuffering toward us, not willing that any should perish but that all should come to repentance.

2 PETER 3:9

As for God, His way is perfect;
The word of the LORD is proven;
He is a shield to all who trust in Him.

PSALM 18:30

Faith comes by hearing, and hearing by the word of God.

ROMANS 10:17

"For as the rain comes down, and the snow
from heaven,
And do not return there,
But water the earth,
And make it bring forth and bud,
That it may give seed to the sower
And bread to the eater,
So shall My word be that goes forth from
My mouth;
It shall not return to Me void,
But it shall accomplish what I please,
And it shall prosper in the thing for which I
sent it."

ISAIAH 55:10–11

51

TEMPTED

Satan tempted even Jesus Himself, and Satan will tempt you. Some temptations will be easily conquered, while others will mean a lengthy and exhausting struggle. Know, however, that God graciously promises to empower you to stand strong against every single temptation you encounter. He also promises to give you a way out of every situation when you are tempted to stray from His path. He doesn't promise that the choice will be easy, but He encourages you to go boldly before Almighty God's throne to request His help. And Jesus guarantees that, there, you will find the help you need, the strength to stand strong.

*No temptation has overtaken you except such as
is common to man; but God is faithful, who will
not allow you to be tempted beyond what you are
able, but with the temptation will also make the
way of escape, that you may be able to bear it.*

1 Corinthians 10:13

*Seeing then that we have a great High Priest
who has passed through the heavens, Jesus the
Son of God, let us hold fast our confession.
For we do not have a High Priest who cannot
sympathize with our weaknesses, but was in all
points tempted as we are, yet without sin. Let us
therefore come boldly to the throne of grace, that
we may obtain mercy and find grace to help in
time of need.*

Hebrews 4:14–16

In all things He had to be made like His brethren, that He might be a merciful and faithful High Priest in things pertaining to God, to make propitiation for the sins of the people. For in that He Himself has suffered, being tempted, He is able to aid those who are tempted.

HEBREWS 2:17–18

Sin shall not have dominion over you, for you are not under law but under grace.

ROMANS 6:14

Let no one say when he is tempted, "I am tempted by God"; for God cannot be tempted by evil, nor does He Himself tempt anyone. But each one is tempted when he is drawn away by his own desires and enticed.

JAMES 1:13–14

He who covers his sins will not prosper,
*   But whoever confesses and forsakes them will*
*   have mercy.*

PROVERBS 28:13

Be sober, be vigilant; because your adversary
the devil walks about like a roaring lion, seeking
whom he may devour. Resist him, steadfast in
the faith, knowing that the same sufferings are
experienced by your brotherhood in the world.

1 PETER 5:8–9

Be strong in the Lord and in the power of His might.
Put on the whole armor of God, that you may be
able to stand against the wiles of the devil. . . .

[Take] the shield of faith with which you
will be able to quench all the fiery darts of the
wicked one.

EPHESIANS 6:10–11, 16

Submit to God. Resist the devil and he will flee
from you. Draw near to God and He will draw
near to you. Cleanse your hands, you sinners;
and purify your hearts, you double-minded. . . .
Humble yourselves in the sight of the Lord, and
He will lift you up.

JAMES 4:7–8, 10

STRESSED

If you're a parent, you know how hard it is to see your child upset and fearful. Similarly, your loving heavenly Father longs for you to be at peace rather than upset, fearful, and stressed. The best way to deal with your stress—to be rid of that stress—is to run to the God of all comfort. One way to do that is by spending time in prayer and focusing on His unshakable love for you, on His good plans for you, and on the peace He longs for you to experience. God keeps His promises, so go to Him. He is waiting for you, and He longs for you to exchange your stress for His peace.

"God so loved the world that He gave His only begotten Son, that whoever believes in Him should not perish but have everlasting life. For God did not send His Son into the world to condemn the world, but that the world through Him might be saved.

"He who believes in Him is not condemned; but he who does not believe is condemned already, because he has not believed in the name of the only begotten Son of God."

JOHN 3:16–18

The LORD builds up Jerusalem;
    He gathers together the outcasts of Israel.
He heals the brokenhearted
    And binds up their wounds.
He counts the number of the stars;
    He calls them all by name.
Great is our Lord, and mighty in power;
    His understanding is infinite.

PSALM 147:2–5

O Lord, You brought my soul up from the grave;
   You have kept me alive, that I should not go
      down to the pit.
Sing praise to the Lord, you saints of His,
   And give thanks at the remembrance of His
      holy name.
For His anger is but for a moment,
   His favor is for life;
   Weeping may endure for a night,
   But joy comes in the morning.

PSALM 30:3–5

"When you pass through the waters, I will be
      with you;
   And through the rivers, they shall not
      overflow you.
   When you walk through the fire, you shall
      not be burned,
   Nor shall the flame scorch you.
For I am the Lord your God,
   The Holy One of Israel, your Savior."

ISAIAH 43:2–3

"For the Lord God will help Me;
    Therefore I will not be disgraced;
    Therefore I have set My face like a flint,
    And I know that I will not be ashamed.
He is near who justifies Me;
    Who will contend with Me?
    Let us stand together.
    Who is My adversary?
    Let him come near Me.
Surely the Lord God will help Me;
    Who is he who will condemn Me?
    Indeed they will all grow old like a garment;
    The moth will eat them up."

ISAIAH 50:7–9

Cast your burden on the LORD,
    And He shall sustain you.

PSALM 55:22

SPIRITUALLY LUKEWARM

Are you feeling rather complacent about your relationship with Jesus? Have life's demands or hurts put your spiritual health on a back burner? Are you just going through the motions of following Jesus? Are you so distracted or burdened that you're hardly even following Him at all? Your yes to any of these questions is an encouraging sign of self-awareness and your dissatisfaction with the spiritual status quo. For a fresh start right now, confess to God your need for Him. Open your Bible and let His truth wash over you and renew your heart and mind. Ask God to reenergize your passion for Him, and recommit to making Him a priority in your life. God can and will reignite the flame of your faith.

*"Be watchful, and strengthen the things which
remain, that are ready to die, for I have not
found your works perfect before God. . . .*

*"I know your works, that you are neither cold
nor hot. I could wish you were cold or hot. So
then, because you are lukewarm, and neither
cold nor hot, I will vomit you out of My mouth."*

REVELATION 3:2, 15–16

*Beware that you do not forget the LORD your
God by not keeping His commandments, His
judgments, and His statutes which I command
you today.*

DEUTERONOMY 8:11

If we had forgotten the name of our God,
  Or stretched out our hands to a foreign god,
Would not God search this out?
  For He knows the secrets of the heart.

PSALM 44:20–21

*Beware, brethren, lest there be in any of you
an evil heart of unbelief in departing from the
living God; but exhort one another daily, while
it is called "Today," lest any of you be hardened
through the deceitfulness of sin.*

HEBREWS 3:12–13

*If, after [these false teachers] have escaped the
pollutions of the world through the knowledge
of the Lord and Savior Jesus Christ, they are
again entangled in them and overcome, the latter
end is worse for them than the beginning. For
it would have been better for them not to have
known the way of righteousness, than having
known it, to turn from the holy commandment
delivered to them.*

2 PETER 2:20–21

*If we confess our sins, He is faithful and just to
forgive us our sins and to cleanse us from all
unrighteousness.*

1 JOHN 1:9

Thus says the LORD:
"Stand in the ways and see,
And ask for the old paths, where the good way is,
And walk in it;
Then you will find rest for your souls."

JEREMIAH 6:16

"Yet from the days of your fathers
    You have gone away from My ordinances
    And have not kept them.
    Return to Me, and I will return to you,"
    Says the LORD *of hosts.*

MALACHI 3:7

TOTALLY EXHAUSTED

The phrase *bone tired* says it well. You can indeed feel physically and emotionally exhausted to the very core, especially when you've been living with difficult and hurtful circumstances. When you find yourself totally spent, turn to the Lord to fill you with His presence, strengthen your heart, and refresh your spirit. Also ask Him to show you how you reached this point of exhaustion and where, for instance, you ran ahead of Him or in absolutely the wrong direction. Ask Him to help you get on a path of restoration and renewal. Take Him up on His invitation to go to Him, "for [His] yoke is easy and [His] burden is light" (Matthew 11:30).

"Take My yoke upon you and learn from Me, for I am gentle and lowly in heart, and you will find rest for your souls. For My yoke is easy and My burden is light."

MATTHEW 11:29–30

Bless the LORD, O my soul;
> *And all that is within me, bless His holy*
> > *name!*

Bless the LORD, O my soul,
> *And forget not all His benefits:*

Who forgives all your iniquities,
> *Who heals all your diseases,*

Who redeems your life from destruction,
> *Who crowns you with lovingkindness and*
> > *tender mercies,*

Who satisfies your mouth with good things,
> *So that your youth is renewed like the eagle's.*

PSALM 103:1–5

*Wait on the L*ORD,

    And keep His way,

    And He shall exalt you to inherit the land;

    When the wicked are cut off, you shall see it.

I have seen the wicked in great power,

    And spreading himself like a native green

      tree.

Yet he passed away, and behold, he was no more;

    Indeed I sought him, but he could not be

      found.

Mark the blameless man, and observe the up-

      right;

    For the future of that man is peace. . . .

*The salvation of the righteous is from the L*ORD;

    He is their strength in the time of trouble.

*And the L*ORD *shall help them and deliver them;*

    He shall deliver them from the wicked,

    And save them,

    Because they trust in Him.

PSALM 37:34–37, 39–40

For thus says the High and Lofty One
   Who inhabits eternity, whose name is Holy:
   "I dwell in the high and holy place,
   With him who has a contrite and humble
      spirit,
   To revive the spirit of the humble,
   And to revive the heart of the contrite
      ones. . . .
"I have seen his ways, and will heal him;
   I will also lead him,
   And restore comforts to him
   And to his mourners.
"I create the fruit of the lips:
   Peace, peace to him who is far off and to him
      who is near,"
   Says the LORD,
   "And I will heal him."

ISAIAH 57:15, 18–19

67

TRUTH

for when you . . .

ARE SUDDENLY OUT OF WORK

The loss of a job can shake a wage earner to the very core. You may have learned that lesson from experience, or you may be experiencing that right now. What are you going to do to pay the bills and feed your family? You might also be wondering why God allowed this job loss to happen. If you are, ask Him, "What do You want me to learn?" One thing God continues to teach all His children is to trust Him. So choose to believe that the Lord knows your needs as well as what is best for you. Turn to Him, spend time with Him, and seek His perfect will for your life. God may have a completely new plan for you. Rest in His presence and choose— moment by moment—to trust Him.

Oh, taste and see that the LORD is good;
    Blessed is the man who trusts in Him!
Oh, fear the LORD, you His saints!
    There is no want to those who fear Him.
The young lions lack and suffer hunger;
    But those who seek the LORD shall not lack
        any good thing.

PSALM 34:8–10

My son, give attention to my words;
    Incline your ear to my sayings.
Do not let them depart from your eyes;
    Keep them in the midst of your heart;
For they are life to those who find them,
    And health to all their flesh.
Keep your heart with all diligence,
    For out of it spring the issues of life.

PROVERBS 4:20–23

O LORD, *You have searched me and known me.*
You know my sitting down and my rising up;
　　You understand my thought afar off.
You comprehend my path and my lying down,
　　And are acquainted with all my ways.
For there is not a word on my tongue,
　　But behold, O LORD, *You know it altogether.*
You have hedged me behind and before,
　　And laid Your hand upon me.
Such knowledge is too wonderful for me;
　　It is high, I cannot attain it.

Where can I go from Your Spirit?
　　Or where can I flee from Your presence?
If I ascend into heaven, You are there;
　　If I make my bed in hell, behold, You are there.
If I take the wings of the morning,
　　And dwell in the uttermost parts of the sea,
Even there Your hand shall lead me,
　　And Your right hand shall hold me.
If I say, "Surely the darkness shall fall on me,"
　　Even the night shall be light about me;

Indeed, the darkness shall not hide from You,
But the night shines as the day;
The darkness and the light are both alike
to You. . . .

Search me, O God, and know my heart;
Try me, and know my anxieties;
And see if there is any wicked way in me,
And lead me in the way everlasting.

PSALM 139:1–12, 23–24

LACK CONFIDENCE

Pain in this world often comes when we place confidence in anyone or anything other than our Sovereign and Good Lord: it is misplaced confidence. Fueling a lack of confidence in yourself can be family challenges, business disappointments, financial pressure, and even a bad night's sleep. In moments like those, you can choose to place your confidence in the almighty God. After all, He has promised to be with you always and in every circumstance. He has promised to never leave you nor forsake you. And He has promised that His strength will be made perfect in your weakness.

[The Lord] said to me [Paul], "My grace is sufficient for you, for my power is made perfect in weakness." Therefore I will boast all the more gladly of my weaknesses, so that the power of Christ may rest upon me.

2 CORINTHIANS 12:9 ESV

Let your conduct be without covetousness; be content with such things as you have. For He Himself has said, "I will never leave you nor forsake you." So we may boldly say:

"The LORD is my helper;
I will not fear.
What can man do to me?"

HEBREWS 13:5–6

The LORD God is my strength;
He will make my feet like deer's feet,
And He will make me walk on my high hills.

HABAKKUK 3:19

The LORD will guide you continually;
  And satisfy your soul in drought,
  And strengthen your bones;
  You shall be like a watered garden,
  And like a spring of water, whose waters do
    not fail.

ISAIAH 58:11

Now this is the confidence that we have in Him,
that if we ask anything according to His will,
He hears us. And if we know that He hears us,
whatever we ask, we know that we have the
petitions that we have asked of Him.

1 JOHN 5:14–15

Do not be afraid of sudden terror,
  Nor of trouble from the wicked when it
    comes;
For the LORD will be your confidence,
  And will keep your foot from being caught.

PROVERBS 3:25–26

If God is for us, who can be against us? He who did not spare His own Son, but delivered Him up for us all, how shall He not with Him also freely give us all things? Who shall bring a charge against God's elect? It is God who justifies. Who is he who condemns? It is Christ who died, and furthermore is also risen, who is even at the right hand of God, who also makes intercession for us. Who shall separate us from the love of Christ? Shall tribulation, or distress, or persecution, or famine, or nakedness, or peril, or sword? . . . In all these things we are more than conquerors through Him who loved us.

ROMANS 8:31–35, 37

I can do all things through Christ who strengthens me.

PHILIPPIANS 4:13

ARE ILL

Often a physical illness will impact you more than just physically. It can impact emotions and hope, your spirit and your soul. But God Himself can redeem even those times for your good and His glory. When you are ill and forced to slow down, of course visit the doctor, take your medicine, and rest. And, yes, pray to the Lord, for He is the One who heals your diseases. Sometimes, though, Jesus also wants to speak to you during this quieter time, so look and listen for what He wants to teach you when you are ill.

Heal me, O Lord, *and I shall be healed;*
  Save me, and I shall be saved,
  For You are my praise.

Jeremiah 17:14

Is anyone among you sick? Let him call for the
elders of the church, and let them pray over him,
anointing him with oil in the name of the Lord.
And the prayer of faith will save the sick, and the
Lord will raise him up. And if he has committed
sins, he will be forgiven.

James 5:14–15

"If you diligently heed the voice of the Lord *your*
God and do what is right in His sight, give ear to
His commandments and keep all His statutes, I
will put none of the diseases on you which I have
brought on the Egyptians. For I am the Lord
who heals you."

Exodus 15:26

Bless the LORD, O my soul,

And forget not all His benefits:

Who forgives all your iniquities,

Who heals all your diseases.

PSALM 103:2-3

[Jesus] Himself bore our sins in His own body on the tree, that we, having died to sins, might live for righteousness—by whose stripes you were healed.

1 PETER 2:24

Surely [Jesus] has borne our griefs

And carried our sorrows;

Yet we esteemed Him stricken,

Smitten by God, and afflicted.

But He was wounded for our transgressions,

He was bruised for our iniquities;

The chastisement for our peace was upon Him,

And by His stripes we are healed.

ISAIAH 53:4–5

The whole multitude sought to touch [Jesus], for power went out from Him and healed them all.

LUKE 6:19

"I will restore health to you
 And heal you of your wounds," says
  the LORD.

JEREMIAH 30:17

FACE FINANCIAL PROBLEMS

Financial difficulties can turn your focus inward and build up incredible stress, worry, and anxiety. You can feel suffocated by outstanding bills and preoccupied about how you will ever pay them. Turning to God for wisdom and direction is vital to every step you are taking toward financial freedom. His Word is filled with the knowledge and insight you need for getting through these tough times. He knows your needs and will provide in ways you can't even imagine. He has promised to supply all your needs according to the riches of His perfect knowledge, unlimited power, and unshakable love for you.

*"Do not worry, saying, 'What shall we eat?' or
'What shall we drink?' or 'What shall we wear?'
For after all these things the Gentiles seek. For
your heavenly Father knows that you need all
these things. But seek first the kingdom of God
and His righteousness, and all these things shall
be added to you."*

MATTHEW 6:31–33

*Now to Him who is able to do exceedingly
abundantly above all that we ask or think,
according to the power that works in us.*

EPHESIANS 3:20

*The young lions lack and suffer hunger;
    But those who seek the LORD shall not lack
        any good thing.*

PSALM 34:10

"Give, and it will be given to you: good measure, pressed down, shaken together, and running over will be put into your bosom. For with the same measure that you use, it will be measured back to you."

Luke 6:38

This I say: He who sows sparingly will also reap sparingly, and he who sows bountifully will also reap bountifully. So let each one give as he purposes in his heart, not grudgingly or of necessity; for God loves a cheerful giver. And God is able to make all grace abound toward you, that you, always having all sufficiency in all things, may have an abundance for every good work.

2 Corinthians 9:6–8

My God shall supply all your need according to His riches in glory by Christ Jesus.

Philippians 4:19

I have been young, and now am old;
    Yet I have not seen the righteous forsaken,
    Nor his descendants begging bread.
He is ever merciful, and lends;
    And his descendants are blessed.

PSALM 37:25–26

"Be strong and very courageous, that you may observe to do according to all the law which Moses My servant commanded you; do not turn from it to the right hand or to the left, that you may prosper wherever you go. This Book of the Law shall not depart from your mouth, but you shall meditate in it day and night, that you may observe to do according to all that is written in it."

JOSHUA 1:7–8

TRUTH FOR WHEN YOU . . .
STRUGGLE IN YOUR MARRIAGE

Statistics about failed marriages—both inside and outside the church—offer tragic evidence that marriage is difficult. But the Bible is filled with proven wisdom, sound hope, and godly encouragement for standing strong in marriage. There must be not only a lasting commitment to each other, but an active, thriving relationship with God.

God's Word clearly states that a husband is to love his wife as he loves himself, and a wife is to respect her husband—but doing this in your own power will lead to frustration and failure. Ask the Lord to help both of you love and respect each other—and He will.

All of you be of one mind, having compassion for
one another; love as brothers, be tenderhearted,
be courteous; not returning evil for evil or
reviling for reviling, but on the contrary blessing,
knowing that you were called to this, that you
may inherit a blessing. For

"He who would love life
And see good days,
Let him refrain his tongue from evil,
And his lips from speaking deceit.
Let him turn away from evil and do good;
Let him seek peace and pursue it."

1 Peter 3:8–11

A man shall leave his father and mother and
be joined to his wife, and they shall become one
flesh.

Genesis 2:24

*Wives, submit to your own husbands, as to the
Lord. For the husband is head of the wife, as also
Christ is head of the church; and He is the Savior
of the body. Therefore, just as the church is
subject to Christ, so let the wives be to their own
husbands in everything.*

*Husbands, love your wives, just as Christ
also loved the church and gave Himself for
her, that He might sanctify and cleanse her with
the washing of water by the word, that He might
present her to Himself a glorious church, not
having spot or wrinkle or any such thing, but
that she should be holy and without blemish. So
husbands ought to love their own wives as their
own bodies; he who loves his wife loves himself.
For no one ever hated his own flesh, but nour-
ishes and cherishes it, just as the Lord does the
church. For we are members of His body, of His
flesh and of His bones.*

Ephesians 5:22–30

Let all bitterness, wrath, anger, clamor, and evil speaking be put away from you, with all malice. And be kind to one another, tenderhearted, forgiving one another, even as God in Christ forgave you.

 EPHESIANS 4:31–32

If it seems evil to you to serve the LORD, choose for yourselves this day whom you will serve, whether the gods which your fathers served that were on the other side of the River, or the gods of the Amorites, in whose land you dwell. But as for me and my house, we will serve the LORD.

JOSHUA 24:15

ARE DISAPPOINTED BY YOUR CHILDREN

Your children are precious, and you want the best for them. You desire that they grow up to love the Lord and be fruitful in life. Unfortunately, your children will disappoint you. Be patient with them just as God, your heavenly Father, is patient with you. When you're disappointed by your children, your love for them reflects God's love for them. Your love for your children will also enable you to help them face their mistakes and the consequences that follow. Turn to God for His wisdom and guidance as you seek to discipline and correct your children. Remember, the primary goal is to steer them back to the path that leads straight to Jesus.

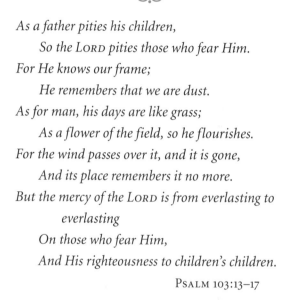

As a father pities his children,
    So the LORD pities those who fear Him.
For He knows our frame;
    He remembers that we are dust.
As for man, his days are like grass;
    As a flower of the field, so he flourishes.
For the wind passes over it, and it is gone,
    And its place remembers it no more.
But the mercy of the LORD is from everlasting to
        everlasting
    On those who fear Him,
    And His righteousness to children's children.

PSALM 103:13–17

Fathers, do not provoke your children to
wrath, but bring them up in the training and
admonition of the Lord.

EPHESIANS 6:4

"If his sons forsake My law
    And do not walk in My judgments,
If they break My statutes
    And do not keep My commandments,
Then I will punish their transgression with
        the rod,
    And their iniquity with stripes.
Nevertheless My lovingkindness I will not utterly
        take from him,
    Nor allow My faithfulness to fail.
My covenant I will not break,
    Nor alter the word that has gone out of
        My lips."

PSALM 89:30–34

Foolishness is bound up in the heart of a child;
    The rod of correction will drive it far
        from him.

PROVERBS 22:15

You, O Lord, are a God full of compassion,
and gracious,
Longsuffering and abundant in mercy
and truth.
Oh, turn to me, and have mercy on me!
Give Your strength to Your servant,
And save the son of Your maidservant.

PSALM 86:15–16

Many times [the LORD] delivered them;
But they rebelled in their counsel,
And were brought low for their iniquity.
Nevertheless He regarded their affliction,
When He heard their cry;
And for their sake He remembered His covenant,
And relented according to the multitude of
His mercies.

PSALM 106:43–45

Even a child is known by his deeds,
Whether what he does is pure and right.

PROVERBS 20:11

ARE ABANDONED BY A LOVED ONE

Trust can take a long time to grow and solidify, yet it can disappear in an instant. And you may be dealing with the pain of having someone you loved and trusted abandon or betray you. As you grieve your loss, remember that the God of all comfort, your compassionate God, is at your side. He has promised that He will never leave you nor forsake you. Turn to your heavenly Father, rest in His presence, and believe His commitment to love you with an everlasting love. Since God is for you, who can be against you?

*Be strong and of good courage, do not fear nor be
afraid of them; for the L*ORD *your God, He is the
One who goes with you. He will not leave you nor
forsake you.*

D<small>EUTERONOMY</small> 31:6

*The L*ORD *also will be a refuge for the oppressed,
    A refuge in times of trouble.
And those who know Your name will put their
        trust in You;
    For You, L*ORD*, have not forsaken those who
    seek You.*

P<small>SALM</small> 9:9–10

*When you turn to the L*ORD *your God and obey
His voice (for the L*ORD *your God is a merciful
God), He will not forsake you nor destroy you,
nor forget the covenant of your fathers which He
swore to them.*

D<small>EUTERONOMY</small> 4:30–31

*Hear, O L*ORD, *when I cry with my voice! . . .*
Do not hide Your face from me;
    Do not turn Your servant away in anger;
    You have been my help;
    Do not leave me nor forsake me,
    O God of my salvation.
When my father and my mother forsake me,
    *Then the L*ORD *will take care of me.*

PSALM 27:7, 9–10

Why are you cast down, O my soul?
    And why are you disquieted within me?
    Hope in God;
    For I shall yet praise Him,
    The help of my countenance and my God.

PSALM 43:5

*The L*ORD *will not forsake His people, for His*
great name's sake, because it has pleased the
L*ORD to make you His people.*

1 SAMUEL 12:22

"*Because he has set his love upon Me, therefore I will deliver him;*
I will set him on high, because he has known My name.
He shall call upon Me, and I will answer him;
I will be with him in trouble;
I will deliver him and honor him."

PSALM 91:14–15

"*Can a woman forget her nursing child,*
And not have compassion on the son of her womb?
Surely they may forget,
Yet I will not forget you.
See, I have inscribed you on the palms of My hands;
Your walls are continually before Me."

ISAIAH 49:15–16

The LORD will not cast off His people,
Nor will He forsake His inheritance.

PSALM 94:14

ARE WAITING ON THE LORD

Waiting on the Lord isn't easy. Your natural—very human—tendency is to want all your problems solved and all your needs met immediately. Have you ever thought, though, about why God has you waiting, and what His purpose might be? Perhaps God is trying to get your attention, teach you something about Himself, or smooth some of your rough edges. The psalmist probably didn't like waiting, but he had learned that when you "wait on the LORD . . . He shall strengthen your heart" (Psalm 27:14). May this promise encourage you to look to God and lean on Him as you wait. Remember that your heavenly Father always knows what is best for you and when.

My soul, wait silently for God alone,
For my expectation is from Him.
He only is my rock and my salvation;
He is my defense;
I shall not be moved.
In God is my salvation and my glory;
The rock of my strength,
And my refuge, is in God.

PSALM 62:5–7

Our soul waits for the LORD;
He is our help and our shield.
For our heart shall rejoice in Him,
Because we have trusted in His holy name.
Let Your mercy, O LORD, be upon us,
Just as we hope in You.

PSALM 33:20–22

Those who wait on the LORD
  Shall renew their strength;
  They shall mount up with wings like eagles,
  They shall run and not be weary,
  They shall walk and not faint.

ISAIAH 40:31

I wait for the LORD, my soul waits,
  And in His word I do hope.
My soul waits for the Lord
  More than those who watch for the
    morning—
  Yes, more than those who watch for the
    morning.

PSALM 130:5–6

Wait on the LORD;
  Be of good courage,
  And He shall strengthen your heart;
  Wait, I say, on the LORD!

PSALM 27:14

It will be said in that day:
   "Behold, this is our God;
   We have waited for Him, and He will save us.
   This is the LORD;
   We have waited for Him;
   We will be glad and rejoice in His salvation."

ISAIAH 25:9

We have become partakers of Christ if we hold the beginning of our confidence steadfast to the end.

HEBREWS 3:14

STRUGGLE TO FORGIVE
SOMEONE

Every single one of God's commands is good for us, and He clearly commands us to forgive people (Luke 17:3–4). If obeying God isn't reason enough to forgive, realize that when you harbor anger and resentment toward someone, you are hardening your heart. Too much of that can make your heart impenetrable, even by God's love. A wise but anonymous source once observed, "Not forgiving is like drinking poison and expecting the other person to die." So, yes, acknowledge your feelings, but at the same time look beyond your circumstances to your holy and forgiving God. He can and will enable you to forgive the person who has hurt you.

As the elect of God, holy and beloved, put on tender mercies, kindness, humility, meekness, longsuffering; bearing with one another, and forgiving one another, if anyone has a complaint against another; even as Christ forgave you, so you also must do. But above all these things put on love, which is the bond of perfection.

COLOSSIANS 3:12–14

"If you forgive men their trespasses, your heavenly Father will also forgive you. But if you do not forgive men their trespasses, neither will your Father forgive your trespasses."

MATTHEW 6:14–15

We know Him who said, "Vengeance is Mine, I will repay," says the Lord. And again, "The LORD will judge His people."

HEBREWS 10:30

Peter came to [Jesus] and said, "Lord, how often shall my brother sin against me, and I forgive him? Up to seven times?"

Jesus said to him, "I do not say to you, up to seven times, but up to seventy times seven."

MATTHEW 18:21–22

"If your brother sins against you, rebuke him; and if he repents, forgive him. And if he sins against you seven times in a day, and seven times in a day returns to you, saying, 'I repent,' you shall forgive him."

LUKE 17:3–4

"Whenever you stand praying, if you have anything against anyone, forgive him, that your Father in heaven may also forgive you your trespasses. But if you do not forgive, neither will your Father in heaven forgive your trespasses."

MARK 11:25–26

"Blessed are those who are persecuted for
                righteousness' sake,
    For theirs is the kingdom of heaven.
"Blessed are you when they revile and persecute
you, and say all kinds of evil against you falsely
for My sake. Rejoice and be exceedingly glad, for
great is your reward in heaven, for so they perse-
cuted the prophets who were before you."

MATTHEW 5:10–12

WANT TO GROW SPIRITUALLY

Growing in your knowledge of Jesus Christ is essential to your walk with God. He wants you to learn more about Him, His Word, and His Son, Jesus, throughout your life. But walking closely with Jesus and being filled with knowledge and wisdom happens only when you read God's Word. Getting to know Him better will also help you be more sensitive to His leading. And following Him throughout your life—obeying His commands and walking according to His ways—will bless you as well as glorify Him. Your desire to grow spiritually is very much in line with God's will, and as you do your part, He will do His.

Add to your faith virtue, to virtue knowledge, to knowledge self-control, to self-control perseverance, to perseverance godliness, to godliness brotherly kindness, and to brotherly kindness love. For if these things are yours and abound, you will be neither barren nor unfruitful in the knowledge of our Lord Jesus Christ.

2 PETER 1:5–8

Grow in the grace and knowledge of our Lord and Savior Jesus Christ.

To Him be the glory both now and forever. Amen.

2 PETER 3:18

As newborn babes, desire the pure milk of the word, that you may grow thereby, if indeed you have tasted that the Lord is gracious.

1 PETER 2:2–3

*Be an example to the believers in word,
in conduct, in love, in spirit, in faith, in
purity. . . . Meditate on these things; give yourself
entirely to them, that your progress may be
evident to all. Take heed to yourself and to the
doctrine. Continue in them, for in doing this you
will save both yourself and those who hear you.*

1 TIMOTHY 4:12, 15–16

*I bow my knees to the Father of our Lord Jesus
Christ, from whom the whole family in heaven
and earth is named, that He would grant
you, according to the riches of His glory, to be
strengthened with might through His Spirit in
the inner man, that Christ may dwell in your
hearts through faith; that you, being rooted and
grounded in love, may be able to comprehend
with all the saints what is the width and length
and depth and height—to know the love of
Christ which passes knowledge; that you may be
filled with all the fullness of God.*

EPHESIANS 3:14–19

Be diligent to present yourself approved to God, a worker who does not need to be ashamed, rightly dividing the word of truth.

2 TIMOTHY 2:15

The Lord is the Spirit; and where the Spirit of the Lord is, there is liberty. But we all, with unveiled face, beholding as in a mirror the glory of the Lord, are being transformed into the same image from glory to glory, just as by the Spirit of the Lord.

2 CORINTHIANS 3:17–18

NEED TO SURRENDER TO GOD

Have you ever thought about what it means to completely surrender yourself to God? That word *surrender* suggests not having control over your life, and that sounds scary. But when you surrender yourself to God, His blessings can flow into your life. So whenever you find yourself desiring material things or status in this world, shift mental gears. Choose to surrender your thoughts to God. Choose to praise Him, open your Bible, or pray. Surrendering yourself—your heart, your thoughts, every minute of your day—to God is your choice. It's a choice God will help you live out. And it's a choice He will bless.

Without faith it is impossible to please Him, for he who comes to God must believe that He is, and that He is a rewarder of those who diligently seek Him.

HEBREWS 11:6

Present your bodies a living sacrifice, holy, acceptable to God, which is your reasonable service. And do not be conformed to this world, but be transformed by the renewing of your mind, that you may prove what is that good and acceptable and perfect will of God.

ROMANS 12:1–2

If you forsake the LORD and serve foreign gods, then He will turn and do you harm and consume you, after He has done you good.

JOSHUA 24:20

"Everyone who is called by My name,
    Whom I have created for My glory;
    I have formed him, yes, I have made him. . . .
"This people I have formed for Myself;
    They shall declare My praise."

ISAIAH 43:7, 21

"The hour is coming, and now is, when the true
worshipers will worship the Father in spirit and
truth; for the Father is seeking such to worship
Him. God is Spirit, and those who worship Him
must worship in spirit and truth."

JOHN 4:23–24

Let us continually offer the sacrifice of praise to
God, that is, the fruit of our lips, giving thanks
to His name. But do not forget to do good and to
share, for with such sacrifices God is well pleased.

HEBREWS 13:15–16

You also, as living stones, are being built up a spiritual house, a holy priesthood, to offer up spiritual sacrifices acceptable to God through Jesus Christ. . . .

You are a chosen generation, a royal priesthood, a holy nation, His own special people, that you may proclaim the praises of Him who called you out of darkness into His marvelous light.

1 PETER 2:5, 9

I exhort first of all that supplications, prayers, intercessions, and giving of thanks be made for all men . . . for this is good and acceptable in the sight of God our Savior . . .

I desire therefore that the men pray everywhere, lifting up holy hands, without wrath and doubting.

1 TIMOTHY 2:1, 3, 8

NEED GOD'S PROTECTION

When you are feeling attacked on every side, let God be your safe haven. There is no better place to turn than to the One who has promised to be your shield, your sanctuary, your light, and your strength. Call on Him in prayer and then choose to rest in His promise of protection. Your God is sovereign—the supreme authority over your life—and He is all-powerful, far greater than any negative force you will ever face. Seek refuge and protection in Him and discover both today and over your lifetime that "blessed is the man who trusts in Him" (Psalm 34:8).

The Lord is my light and my salvation;
  Whom shall I fear?
  The Lord is the strength of my life;
  Of whom shall I be afraid? . . .
For in the time of trouble
  He shall hide me in His pavilion;
  In the secret place of His tabernacle
  He shall hide me;
  He shall set me high upon a rock.

PSALM 27:1, 5

I will both lie down in peace, and sleep;
  For You alone, O Lord, make me dwell in
    safety.

PSALM 4:8

The fear of man brings a snare;
  But whoever trusts in the Lord shall be safe.

PROVERBS 29:25

He who dwells in the secret place of the
        Most High
    Shall abide under the shadow of the
        Almighty.
I will say of the Lord, *"He is my refuge and*
        my fortress;
    My God, in Him I will trust."
Surely He shall deliver you from the snare of
        the fowler
    And from the perilous pestilence.
He shall cover you with His feathers,
    And under His wings you shall take refuge;
    His truth shall be your shield and buckler.
You shall not be afraid of the terror by night,
    Nor of the arrow that flies by day,
Nor of the pestilence that walks in darkness,
    Nor of the destruction that lays waste at
        noonday.
A thousand may fall at your side,
    And ten thousand at your right hand;
    But it shall not come near you.

Psalm 91:1–7

Let all those rejoice who put their trust in You;
  Let them ever shout for joy, because You
    defend them;
  Let those also who love Your name
  Be joyful in You.
For You, O Lord, will bless the righteous;
  With favor You will surround him as
    with a shield.

Psalm 5:11–12

The angel of the Lord encamps all around those
    who fear Him,
  And delivers them.
Oh, taste and see that the Lord is good;
  Blessed is the man who trusts in Him!

Psalm 34: 7–8

FACE DISAPPOINTMENT
IN LIFE

D isappointment is a part of life—and no one is immune to its effects. So when life brings disappointment, the best comfort you can find will be in the arms of your heavenly Father. He provides reassurance and understanding no other source can. And the good news is, He promises to save you, revive you, and "perfect that which concerns [you]" (Psalm 138:8). It's important to acknowledge and grieve disappointments when they come, but it's also important to move forward by finding comfort in God's promises of hope and joy that transcend this world and its heartache. He is always ready to console and encourage you. Make a point to reach out and receive Him.

*In this you greatly rejoice, though now for a
little while, if need be, you have been grieved
by various trials, that the genuineness of your
faith, being much more precious than gold that
perishes, though it is tested by fire, may be found
to praise, honor, and glory at the revelation of
Jesus Christ, whom having not seen you love.
Though now you do not see Him, yet believing,
you rejoice with joy inexpressible and full of
glory, receiving the end of your faith—the
salvation of your souls.*

1 PETER 1:6–9

*We are hard-pressed on every side, yet not
crushed; we are perplexed, but not in despair;
persecuted, but not forsaken; struck down, but
not destroyed—always carrying about in the
body the dying of the Lord Jesus, that the life of
Jesus also may be manifested in our body.*

2 CORINTHIANS 4:8–10

*[Be] confident of this very thing, that He who has
begun a good work in you will complete it until
the day of Jesus Christ.*

PHILIPPIANS 1:6

*The Spirit Himself bears witness with our spirit
that we are children of God, and if children, then
heirs—heirs of God and joint heirs with Christ, if
indeed we suffer with Him, that we may also be
glorified together.*

*For I consider that the sufferings of this pres-
ent time are not worthy to be compared with the
glory which shall be revealed in us.*

ROMANS 8:16–18

*The LORD is near to those who have a broken
        heart,
    And saves such as have a contrite spirit.
Many are the afflictions of the righteous,
        But the LORD delivers him out of them all.*

PSALM 34:18–19

The steps of a good man are ordered by the LORD,
  And He delights in his way.
Though he fall, he shall not be utterly cast down;
  For the LORD upholds him with His hand.
I have been young, and now am old;
  Yet I have not seen the righteous forsaken,
  Nor his descendants begging bread.
He is ever merciful, and lends;
  And his descendants are blessed.

PSALM 37:23–26

The LORD will perfect that which concerns me;
  Your mercy, O LORD, endures forever;
  Do not forsake the works of Your hands.

PSALM 138:8

"For the mountains shall depart
  And the hills be removed,
  But My kindness shall not depart from you,
  Nor shall My covenant of peace be removed,"
Says the LORD, who has mercy on you.

ISAIAH 54:10

HAVE BEEN BETRAYED

Perhaps nothing is as devastating as being betrayed by someone you loved and trusted, by someone you thought loved you. Know that Jesus—betrayed by Judas, denied by Peter—fully understands. He will enable you to recover, and the key, as hard as it is, is to pray for that person and ask God to bless him or her. When you do—and you'll have to pray this again and again—you release the anger and disappointment that come with being betrayed. Retaliating is a natural response, but it's not a godly response; neither is gossiping to rally support. Praying is always the best option. Allow the Lord to receive your hurt and anger, and to replace them with His peace that passes understanding.

Love suffers long and is kind; love does not envy;
love does not parade itself, is not puffed up; does not
behave rudely, does not seek its own, is not provoked,
thinks no evil . . . bears all things, believes all things,
hopes all things, endures all things.

1 Corinthians 13:4–5

You, O Lord, are a shield for me,
    My glory and the One who lifts up my head.
I cried to the Lord with my voice,
    And He heard me from His holy hill. Selah
I lay down and slept;
    I awoke, for the Lord sustained me.
I will not be afraid of ten thousands of people
    Who have set themselves against me all around.

Psalm 3:3–6

All of you be of one mind, having compassion for one another; love as brothers, be tenderhearted, be courteous; not returning evil for evil or reviling for reviling, but on the contrary blessing, knowing that you were called to this, that you may inherit a blessing. For

> *"He who would love life*
>> *And see good days,*
>> *Let him refrain his tongue from evil,*
>> *And his lips from speaking deceit.*
> *Let him turn away from evil and do good;*
>> *Let him seek peace and pursue it.*
> *For the eyes of the* Lord *are on the righteous,*
>> *And His ears are open to their prayers;*
>> *But the face of the* Lord *is against those*
>>> *who do evil."*

1 Peter 3:8–12

Be of the same mind toward one another. Do not set your mind on high things, but associate with the humble. Do not be wise in your own opinion.

Repay no one evil for evil. Have regard for good things in the sight of all men. If it is possible, as much as depends on you, live peaceably with all men. Beloved, do not avenge yourselves, but rather give place to wrath; for it is written, "Vengeance is Mine, I will repay," says the Lord.

ROMANS 12:16–19

"Be merciful, just as your Father also is merciful.

"Judge not, and you shall not be judged. Condemn not, and you shall not be condemned. Forgive, and you will be forgiven."

LUKE 6:36–37

ARE FACING THE REALITY
OF GETTING OLDER

Realizing that you're getting older can be jarring. After all, you probably still feel like you're eighteen or twenty-five or thirty-five . . . But give thanks to God that these years are part of His good plan for you. Choose to celebrate how the Lord has shaped your life for your good and for His glory. And acknowledge before the Lord that He has promised that you will "bear fruit in old age" (Psalm 92:14). Ask Him to show you where and how to do exactly that, and He will. You might, for instance, share your life with someone younger. Being a mentor will mean blessings for you and blessings for those you come alongside as you share with them your wisdom and love.

*Bless the L*ORD*, O my soul;*
*   And all that is within me, bless His holy*
*   name!*
*Bless the L*ORD*, O my soul,*
*   And forget not all His benefits:*
Who forgives all your iniquities,
*   Who heals all your diseases,*
Who redeems your life from destruction,
*   Who crowns you with lovingkindness and*
*   tender mercies,*
Who satisfies your mouth with good things,
*   So that your youth is renewed like the eagle's.*

PSALM 103:1–5

None of us lives to himself, and no one dies to
himself. For if we live, we live to the Lord; and if
we die, we die to the Lord. Therefore, whether we
live or die, we are the Lord's.

ROMANS 14:7–8

The righteous shall flourish like a palm tree,
He shall grow like a cedar in Lebanon.
Those who are planted in the house of the LORD
Shall flourish in the courts of our God.
They shall still bear fruit in old age;
They shall be fresh and flourishing,
To declare that the LORD *is upright;*
He is my rock, and there is no
unrighteousness in Him.

PSALM 92:12–15

The days of our lives are seventy years;
And if by reason of strength they are eighty
years,
Yet their boast is only labor and sorrow;
For it is soon cut off, and we fly away. . . .
So teach us to number our days,
That we may gain a heart of wisdom. . . .
Oh, satisfy us early with Your mercy,
That we may rejoice and be glad all our days!

PSALM 90:10, 12, 14

I know that my Redeemer lives,

*   And He shall stand at last on the earth;*
And after my skin is destroyed, this I know,

*   That in my flesh I shall see God,*
Whom I shall see for myself,

*   And my eyes shall behold, and not another.*
*   How my heart yearns within me!*

                                        JOB 19:25–27

We do not lose heart. Even though our outward
man is perishing, yet the inward man is being
renewed day by day. For our light affliction,
which is but for a moment, is working for us a far
more exceeding and eternal weight of glory, while
we do not look at the things which are seen, but
at the things which are not seen. For the things
which are seen are temporary, but the things
which are not seen are eternal.

                              2 CORINTHIANS 4:16–18

WANT TO GIVE UP

We've all experienced times when circumstances are overwhelming, people are difficult, and relationships seem hopeless. Beat down, you just want to throw up your hands in defeat. When you find yourself in a place like that, remember that you are not alone. Despite what your feelings may suggest, God—the One for whom nothing is impossible—is with you and He goes before you. You may feel discouraged, but God will give you the strength and wisdom you need to endure the next moment, the next hour, the next day. God knows your circumstances, your hurts, and your frustrations, and He will never leave you to face them alone. Ask Him for His strength and rest in His presence with you.

*Seeing then that we have a great High Priest
who has passed through the heavens, Jesus the
Son of God, let us hold fast our confession.
For we do not have a High Priest who cannot
sympathize with our weaknesses, but was in all
points tempted as we are, yet without sin. Let us
therefore come boldly to the throne of grace, that
we may obtain mercy and find grace to help in
time of need.*

HEBREWS 4:14–16

*I have learned in whatever state I am, to be
content: I know how to be abased, and I know
how to abound. Everywhere and in all things I
have learned both to be full and to be hungry,
both to abound and to suffer need. I can do all
things through Christ who strengthens me.*

PHILIPPIANS 4:11–13

"Fear not, for I am with you;
    Be not dismayed, for I am your God.
    I will strengthen you,
    Yes, I will help you,
    I will uphold you with My righteous
        right hand."

ISAIAH 41:10

Thanks be to God, who gives us the victory through our Lord Jesus Christ.
    Therefore, my beloved brethren, be steadfast, immovable, always abounding in the work of the Lord, knowing that your labor is not in vain in the Lord.

1 CORINTHIANS 15:57–58

Consider Him who endured such hostility from sinners against Himself, lest you become weary and discouraged in your souls.

HEBREWS 12:3

"Behold, I have created the blacksmith
	Who blows the coals in the fire,
	Who brings forth an instrument for his work;
	And I have created the spoiler to destroy.
No weapon formed against you shall prosper,
	And every tongue which rises against
		you in judgment
	You shall condemn.
	This is the heritage of the servants of the
		LORD,
	And their righteousness is from Me,"
	Says the LORD.

ISAIAH 54:16–17

133

NEED PATIENCE

Perhaps when you think about your need for patience, you think about challenging people rather than situations. But whether you're feeling impatient with a person, a trial, or even God Himself, remember that He is sovereign, which means that those people and situations didn't randomly fall into your life. At the very least, they give you an opportunity to look to God and grow in His grace. Ask your heavenly Father to give you the patience you need, patience He wants to give you. Recite a promise from Scripture. And choose to trust that He will use for your growth in Christlikeness whatever is causing you to feel impatient.

*Count it all joy when you fall into various trials,
knowing that the testing of your faith produces
patience. But let patience have its perfect work,
that you may be perfect and complete, lacking
nothing.*

JAMES 1:2–4

*Rest in the L<small>ORD</small>, and wait patiently for Him;
    Do not fret because of him who prospers in
        his way,
    Because of the man who brings wicked
        schemes to pass.
Cease from anger, and forsake wrath;
    Do not fret—it only causes harm. . . .
The L<small>ORD</small> knows the days of the upright,
    And their inheritance shall be forever.*

PSALM 37:7–8, 18

When you do good and suffer, if you take it
patiently, this is commendable before God. For to
this you were called, because Christ also suffered
for us, leaving us an example, that you should
follow His steps.

1 PETER 2:20–21

Consider the work of God;
    For who can make straight what He has
        made crooked?
In the day of prosperity be joyful,
    But in the day of adversity consider:
    Surely God has appointed the one as well as
        the other,
    So that man can find out nothing that will
        come after him.

ECCLESIASTES 7:13–14

*Since we are surrounded by so great a cloud
of witnesses, let us lay aside every weight, and
the sin which so easily ensnares us, and let us
run with endurance the race that is set before
us, looking unto Jesus, the author and finisher of
our faith, who for the joy that was set before Him
endured the cross, despising the shame, and has
sat down at the right hand of the throne of God.*

HEBREWS 12:1–2

*Whatever things were written before were
written for our learning, that we through the
patience and comfort of the Scriptures might
have hope. Now may the God of patience and
comfort grant you to be like-minded toward one
another, according to Christ Jesus.*

ROMANS 15:4–5

FACE A CRISIS

On this side of heaven, you may never understand why God allows you to experience certain tough times, unexpected hurts, or devastating setbacks. But trying to figure out God and His reasons is an exercise in futility. His ways are not like your ways (Isaiah 55:8). But you can be sure that He is all-powerful, all-loving, all-wise, and all-good. Whether you are in a season of calm or crisis, God is with you. So when you face a crisis, go to Him in prayer and ask Him to lead you, guide you, even carry you. Your almighty God has promised to answer you whenever you call upon Him; He has promised to be with you in times of trouble. You can rely on His promises. On every single one.

"Fear not, for I have redeemed you;
     I have called you by your name;
     You are Mine.
When you pass through the waters, I will be
          with you;
     And through the rivers, they shall not
          overflow you.
     When you walk through the fire, you shall
          not be burned,
     Nor shall the flame scorch you.
For I am the Lord your God,
     The Holy One of Israel, your Savior."

ISAIAH 43:1–3

I will call upon God,
     And the Lord shall save me.
Evening and morning and at noon
     I will pray, and cry aloud,
     And He shall hear my voice.

PSALM 55:16–17

Give ear, O Lord, to my prayer;
　　And attend to the voice of my supplications.
In the day of my trouble I will call upon You,
　　For You will answer me.
Among the gods there is none like You, O Lord;
　　Nor are there any works like Your works.
All nations whom You have made
　　Shall come and worship before You, O Lord,
　　And shall glorify Your name.
For You are great, and do wondrous things;
　　You alone are God.

PSALM 86:6–10

[Cast] all your care upon Him, for He cares for you.
　　Be sober, be vigilant; because your adversary the
devil walks about like a roaring lion, seeking whom
he may devour. Resist him, steadfast in the faith,
knowing that the same sufferings are experienced
by your brotherhood in the world. But may the God
of all grace, who called us to His eternal glory by
Christ Jesus, after you have suffered a while, perfect,
establish, strengthen, and settle you.

1 PETER 5:7–10

I sought the L<small>ORD</small>, *and He heard me,*
And delivered me from all my fears.
They looked to Him and were radiant,
And their faces were not ashamed.
This poor man cried out, and the L<small>ORD</small>
heard him,
And saved him out of all his troubles.
The angel of the L<small>ORD</small> *encamps all around those*
who fear Him,
And delivers them.
Oh, taste and see that the L<small>ORD</small> *is good;*
Blessed is the man who trusts in Him!

P<small>SALM</small> 34:4–8

TRUTH

from the Bible about . . .

GOD'S PLAN FOR YOUR LIFE

Your inability to understand what is happening in your life and why does not negate the truth that God has a plan for you, a plan "to give you a future and a hope" (Jeremiah 29:11). Grab on to that promise and perhaps even consider it a promise of adventure. Walk in the truth of that promise and entrust your future to God. Ask Him how He wants to use you for His glory, then ask Him to help you sense His guidance for your next steps. Rely on Him each day for courage to do what He calls you to do with your time, talents, and treasure. As a Christian, your life is not your own. It belongs to the One who created you and who has a plan just for you.

I know the thoughts that I think toward you, says the LORD, *thoughts of peace and not of evil, to give you a future and a hope. Then you will call upon Me and go and pray to Me, and I will listen to you. And you will seek Me and find Me, when you search for Me with all your heart.*

JEREMIAH 29:11–13

Trust in the LORD *with all your heart,*
    And lean not on your own understanding;
In all your ways acknowledge Him,
    And He shall direct your paths.

PROVERBS 3:5–6

Whatever you do, do it heartily, as to the Lord and not to men, knowing that from the Lord you will receive the reward of the inheritance; for you serve the Lord Christ.

COLOSSIANS 3:23–24

Trust in the Lord, and do good;
  Dwell in the land, and feed on His
    faithfulness.
Delight yourself also in the Lord,
  And He shall give you the desires of your heart.
Commit your way to the Lord,
  Trust also in Him,
  And He shall bring it to pass.
He shall bring forth your righteousness as
    the light,
  And your justice as the noonday.

PSALM 37:3–6

Blessed are those who keep my ways.
Hear instruction and be wise,
  And do not disdain it.
Blessed is the man who listens to me,
  Watching daily at my gates,
  Waiting at the posts of my doors.
For whoever finds me finds life,
  And obtains favor from the Lord.

PROVERBS 8:32–35

Serve the Lord with gladness;
    Come before His presence with singing.
Know that the Lord, He is God;
    It is He who has made us, and not we
        ourselves;
    We are His people and the sheep of His
        pasture.
Enter into His gates with thanksgiving,
    And into His courts with praise.
    Be thankful to Him, and bless His name.
For the Lord is good;
    His mercy is everlasting,
    And His truth endures to all generations.

PSALM 100:2–5

"Whoever desires to save his life will lose it, but whoever loses his life for My sake will find it."

MATTHEW 16:25

TRUTH FROM THE BIBLE ABOUT . . .
ANSWERED PRAYER

What an unbelievable privilege, to be able to go before the Creator of the universe, the Sustainer of all life, and the Author of history with our concerns, our dreams, our hurts, our desires. What an indescribable blessing, to be able to pray. Know that God has promised to listen to all of your prayers and answer them according to His love for you (Jeremiah 33:3). His answer might not be the answer you hope for, and He may not respond according to the timetable you would like. A response, however, is what the Lord promises and that response will be guided by His perfect wisdom and His unshakable love for you.

"Ask, and it will be given to you; seek, and you will find; knock, and it will be opened to you. For everyone who asks receives, and he who seeks finds, and to him who knocks it will be opened."

MATTHEW 7:7–8

"If you have faith and do not doubt, you will not only do what was done to the fig tree, but also if you say to this mountain, 'Be removed and be cast into the sea,' it will be done. And whatever things you ask in prayer, believing, you will receive."

MATTHEW 21:21–22

"If two of you agree on earth concerning anything that they ask, it will be done for them by My Father in heaven. For where two or three are gathered together in My name, I am there in the midst of them."

MATTHEW 18:19–20

"I say to you, whoever says to this mountain, 'Be removed and be cast into the sea,' and does not doubt in his heart, but believes that those things he says will be done, he will have whatever he says. Therefore I say to you, whatever things you ask when you pray, believe that you receive them, and you will have them."

MARK 11:23–24

"I say to you, he who believes in Me, the works that I do he will do also; and greater works than these he will do, because I go to My Father. And whatever you ask in My name, that I will do, that the Father may be glorified in the Son. If you ask anything in My name, I will do it."

JOHN 14:12–14

"Whatever you ask the Father in My name He will give you. Until now you have asked nothing in My name. Ask, and you will receive, that your joy may be full."

JOHN 16:23–24

The LORD is near to all who call upon Him,
     To all who call upon Him in truth.
He will fulfill the desire of those who fear Him;
     He also will hear their cry and save them.

PSALM 145:18–19

"Call to Me, and I will answer you, and show
you great and mighty things, which you do not
know."

JEREMIAH 33:3

"When you pray, you shall not be like the
hypocrites. For they love to pray standing in the
synagogues and on the corners of the streets, that
they may be seen by men. Assuredly, I say to you,
they have their reward. But you, when you pray,
go into your room, and when you have shut your
door, pray to your Father who is in the secret
place; and your Father who sees in secret will
reward you openly."

MATTHEW 6:5–6

TRUTH FROM THE BIBLE ABOUT . . .
CONFESSING YOUR SINS

If you are hurting due to the consequences of your sinful behavior, there's only one way to experience complete cleansing and healing, and that is to acknowledge and confess your sins to God. If you don't, they stay in the recesses of your heart and soul. Unconfessed sin will affect your thoughts and actions in ways that will hurt your relationship with God as well as with other people. Confessing sin is not always easy to do, but the results are glorious and freeing: the weight of sin is instantly lifted, and God's healing balm of forgiveness and restoration bring indescribable joy and peace.

I acknowledged my sin to You,
    And my iniquity I have not hidden.
    I said, "I will confess my transgressions to the
        LORD,"
    And You forgave the iniquity of my sin.

PSALM 32:5

For as the heavens are high above the earth,
    So great is His mercy toward those who fear
        Him;
As far as the east is from the west,
    So far has He removed our transgressions
        from us.

PSALM 103:11–12

He who covers his sins will not prosper,
    But whoever confesses and forsakes them will
        have mercy.

PROVERBS 28:13

If you confess with your mouth the Lord Jesus and believe in your heart that God has raised Him from the dead, you will be saved. For with the heart one believes unto righteousness, and with the mouth confession is made unto salvation.

ROMANS 10:9–10

I said: "I pray, LORD God of heaven, O great and awesome God, You who keep Your covenant and mercy with those who love You and observe Your commandments, please let Your ear be attentive and Your eyes open, that You may hear the prayer of Your servant which I pray before You now, day and night, for the children of Israel Your servants, and confess the sins of the children of Israel which we have sinned against You. Both my father's house and I have sinned. We have acted very corruptly against You, and have not kept the commandments, the statutes, nor the ordinances which You commanded Your servant Moses."

NEHEMIAH 1:5–7

We can boldly enter heaven's Most Holy Place
because of the blood of Jesus. . . . Our guilty
consciences have been sprinkled with Christ's
blood to make us clean, and our bodies have been
washed with pure water.

HEBREWS 10:19, 22 NLT

Have mercy upon me, O God,
   According to Your lovingkindness;
   According to the multitude of Your tender
      mercies,
   Blot out my transgressions.
Wash me thoroughly from my iniquity,
   And cleanse me from my sin. . . .
Purge me with hyssop, and I shall be clean;
   Wash me, and I shall be whiter than snow.

PSALM 51:1–2, 7

THE POWER OF GOD'S WORD

Among the many privileges of being God's child is your opportunity to know His Word and His promises. Jesus gives you the Holy Spirit, enabling you to understand Scripture and appropriate its power especially when you are hurting. Memorizing God's Word and meditating on it also enables you to live in His presence and walk in His truth, to be sensitive to His still, small voice and guided along His path for you. If you want to live in an intimate relationship with your heavenly Father, learn His Word and meditate on it throughout your days. Great power comes with knowing God's Word.

The law of the Lord is perfect, converting
   the soul;
   The testimony of the Lord is sure, making
      wise the simple;
The statutes of the Lord are right, rejoicing
   the heart;
   The commandment of the Lord is pure,
      enlightening the eyes;
The fear of the Lord is clean, enduring forever;
   The judgments of the Lord are true and
      righteous altogether.
More to be desired are they than gold,
   Yea, than much fine gold;
   Sweeter also than honey and the honeycomb.
Moreover by them Your servant is warned,
   And in keeping them there is great reward.

PSALM 19:7–11

Let the words of my mouth and the meditation of
    my heart
  Be acceptable in Your sight,
  O LORD, my strength and my Redeemer.

PSALM 19:14

"I have not spoken on My own authority; but the Father who sent Me gave Me a command, what I should say and what I should speak. And I know that His command is everlasting life. Therefore, whatever I speak, just as the Father has told Me, so I speak."

JOHN 12:49–50

All Scripture is given by inspiration of God, and is profitable for doctrine, for reproof, for correction, for instruction in righteousness, that the man of God may be complete, thoroughly equipped for every good work.

2 TIMOTHY 3:16–17

Your word is a lamp to my feet
And a light to my path.

PSALM 119:105

"So shall My word be that goes forth from My
mouth;
It shall not return to Me void,
But it shall accomplish what I please,
And it shall prosper in the thing for which I
sent it."

ISAIAH 55:11

Teach me, O LORD, the way of Your statutes,
And I shall keep it to the end.
Give me understanding, and I shall keep Your law;
Indeed, I shall observe it with my whole
heart.
Make me walk in the path of Your commandments,
For I delight in it.

PSALM 119:33–35

TRUTH FROM THE BIBLE ABOUT . . .

THE IMPORTANCE OF
CHRISTIAN FELLOWSHIP

If you're hurting, you may find this statement hard to believe: you are important to other Christians—to their faith and their growth in Christlikeness—and they are important to you. You gain strength and find encouragement when you spend time with your Christian brothers and sisters. Sharing your struggles with them will result in blessings of care, compassion, and prayer. You, in turn, can supply the same blessings when others are struggling. In His Word, God cautions you not to neglect spending time with fellow believers even when—maybe *especially* when—you are hurting. Whether you're on the giving or the receiving end, He wants to bless you through members of His family.

*Let us consider one another in order to stir
up love and good works, not forsaking the
assembling of ourselves together, as is the manner
of some, but exhorting one another, and so much
the more as you see the Day approaching.*

HEBREWS 10:24–25

*Whoever has this world's goods, and sees his
brother in need, and shuts up his heart from him,
how does the love of God abide in him? . . . My
little children, let us not love in word or in
tongue, but in deed and in truth.*

1 JOHN 3:17–18

*Let the word of Christ dwell in you richly in all
wisdom, teaching and admonishing one another
in psalms and hymns and spiritual songs, singing
with grace in your hearts to the Lord.*

COLOSSIANS 3:16

Walk in love, as Christ also has loved us and given Himself for us, an offering and a sacrifice to God for a sweet-smelling aroma. . . . Speaking to one another in psalms and hymns and spiritual songs, singing and making melody in your heart to the Lord . . . For we are members of His body, of His flesh and of His bones.

EPHESIANS 5:2, 19, 30

"I am no longer in the world, but these are in the world, and I come to You. Holy Father, keep through Your name those whom You have given Me, that they may be one as We are. . . . [May] they all may be one, as You, Father, are in Me, and I in You; that they also may be one in Us, that the world may believe that You sent Me. And the glory which You gave Me I have given them, that they may be one just as We are one: I in them, and You in Me; that they may be made perfect in one, and that the world may know that You have sent Me, and have loved them as You have loved Me."

JOHN 17:11, 21–23

[New believers] continued steadfastly in the apostles' doctrine and fellowship, in the breaking of bread, and in prayers. . . . So continuing daily with one accord in the temple, and breaking bread from house to house, they ate their food with gladness and simplicity of heart, praising God and having favor with all the people. And the Lord added to the church daily those who were being saved.

ACTS 2:42, 46–47

May the God of patience and comfort grant you to be like-minded toward one another, according to Christ Jesus, that you may with one mind and one mouth glorify the God and Father of our Lord Jesus Christ.

ROMANS 15:5–7

REPRESENTING JESUS

It's been said that your life may be the only Bible some people read. In other words, the characteristics of Jesus that people see in you may be the closest they get to learning about His love for them. Even when you're hurting, God may be using your life—what you do, what you say, and how you say it—to lead someone to Him. When you become a Christian, you become an ambassador for Jesus Christ, and His Spirit will enable you to share His love, teach about His forgiving grace, and reveal His loving-kindness. You are the Lord's witness, and even when you're hurting, the light of His love can shine through you so that others see Jesus.

By this we know love, because [Jesus] laid down His life for us. And we also ought to lay down our lives for the brethren. But whoever has this world's goods, and sees his brother in need, and shuts up his heart from him, how does the love of God abide in him?

My little children, let us not love in word or in tongue, but in deed and in truth.

1 JOHN 3:16–18

[Jesus] said to them, "Go into all the world and preach the gospel to every creature."

MARK 16:15

"You shall receive power when the Holy Spirit has come upon you; and you shall be witnesses to Me in Jerusalem, and in all Judea and Samaria, and to the end of the earth."

ACTS 1:8

"You are the salt of the earth; but if the salt loses its flavor, how shall it be seasoned? It is then good for nothing but to be thrown out and trampled underfoot by men.

"You are the light of the world. A city that is set on a hill cannot be hidden. Nor do they light a lamp and put it under a basket, but on a lampstand, and it gives light to all who are in the house. Let your light so shine before men, that they may see your good works and glorify your Father in heaven."

MATTHEW 5:13–16

If a brother or sister is naked and destitute of daily food, and one of you says to them, "Depart in peace, be warmed and filled," but you do not give them the things which are needed for the body, what does it profit? Thus also faith by itself, if it does not have works, is dead.

JAMES 2:15–17

"'I was hungry and you gave Me food; I was thirsty and you gave Me drink; I was a stranger and you took Me in; I was naked and you clothed Me; I was sick and you visited Me; I was in prison and you came to Me.'

"Then the righteous will answer Him, saying, 'Lord, when did we see You hungry and feed You, or thirsty and give You drink? When did we see You a stranger and take You in, or naked and clothe You? Or when did we see You sick, or in prison, and come to You?' And the King will answer and say to them, 'Assuredly, I say to you, inasmuch as you did it to one of the least of these My brethren, you did it to Me.'"

MATTHEW 25:35–40

GOD'S WILL FOR YOUR LIFE

Seasons of pain may raise questions about God's will for your life. But always of utmost importance is living in a way that pleases and glorifies your heavenly Father and His Son, your Savior. And God reveals much about what kind of life that is: love God with all you are (Mark 12:30); love your neighbor (Matthew 22:39); and live out a love that reflects Jesus (1 Corinthians 13). God will enable you to live according to these general commands, and the Holy Spirit will guide you. Rest assured that the Lord will empower you as you earnestly seek to live out His will, to love Him, and to love others.

Your ears shall hear a word behind you, saying,
  "This is the way, walk in it,"
  Whenever you turn to the right hand
  Or whenever you turn to the left.

ISAIAH 30:21

If any of you lacks wisdom, let him ask of God,
who gives to all liberally and without reproach,
and it will be given to him. But let him ask in
faith, with no doubting, for he who doubts is like
a wave of the sea driven and tossed by the wind.

JAMES 1:5–6

When you roam, [God's commands] will lead you;
  When you sleep, they will keep you;
  And when you awake, they will speak
  with you.

PROVERBS 6:22

This Book of the Law shall not depart from your
mouth, but you shall meditate in it day and night,
that you may observe to do according to all that
is written in it. For then you will make your way
prosperous, and then you will have good success.

JOSHUA 1:8

For this is God,
      Our God forever and ever;
      He will be our guide
      Even to death.

PSALM 48:14

All the ways of a man are pure in his own eyes,
      But the LORD weighs the spirits.
Commit your works to the LORD,
      And your thoughts will be established.

PROVERBS 16:2–3

The steps of a good man are ordered by the Lord,
   And He delights in his way.

Psalm 37:23

Trust in the Lord *with all your heart,*
   And lean not on your own understanding;
In all your ways acknowledge Him,
   And He shall direct your paths.

Proverbs 3:5–6

The Lord *will guide you continually,*
   And satisfy your soul in drought,
   And strengthen your bones;
   You shall be like a watered garden,
   And like a spring of water, whose waters do
      not fail.

Isaiah 58:11

THE HOLY SPIRIT

Whenever you are hurting, it's so easy to feel as though you're going through your struggles alone. But remember that God has sent you the Holy Spirit as your constant Companion, Comforter, and Helper. He is with you all the time. God sent Him, who is the Spirit of truth, to reveal what you need to know about God and to bring to remembrance exactly what He wishes you to know in a given moment. God wants you to experience His presence every waking moment.

Ask God to help you be sensitive to the gentle stirrings of the Holy Spirit in your life. You can be confident that His Spirit will bring comfort and guidance along a path of joy-filled days.

"The Helper, the Holy Spirit, whom the Father will send in My name, He will teach you all things, and bring to your remembrance all things that I said to you."

JOHN 14:26

Do you not know that your body is the temple of the Holy Spirit who is in you, whom you have from God, and you are not your own? For you were bought at a price; therefore glorify God in your body and in your spirit, which are God's.

1 CORINTHIANS 6:19–20

"It shall come to pass afterward
    That I will pour out My Spirit on all flesh."

JOEL 2:28

"I will pray the Father, and He will give you another Helper, that He may abide with you forever—the Spirit of truth, whom the world cannot receive, because it neither sees Him nor knows Him; but you know Him, for He dwells with you and will be in you."

JOHN 14:16–17

"When He, the Spirit of truth, has come, He will guide you into all truth; for He will not speak on His own authority, but whatever He hears He will speak; and He will tell you things to come. He will glorify Me, for He will take of what is Mine and declare it to you."

JOHN 16:13–14

Being assembled together with [the apostles
He had chosen], [Jesus] commanded them not
to depart from Jerusalem, but to wait for the
Promise of the Father, "which," He said, "you
have heard from Me; for John truly baptized with
water, but you shall be baptized with the Holy
Spirit not many days from now. . . . You shall
receive power when the Holy Spirit has come
upon you; and you shall be witnesses to Me in
Jerusalem, and in all Judea and Samaria, and to
the end of the earth."

ACTS 1:4–5, 8

BUILDING YOUR FAITH

If you are hurting, God wants to use this time to grow your faith. Like a muscle, the more you exercise faith (and life's hard times give you that opportunity), the stronger your faith becomes.

Your faith also grows when you do whatever God commands. Surrendering control over your life becomes easier as your faith in Jesus grows, and you build that faith by obeying Him and seeing His response to that obedience. So develop the habit of running to the Lord whenever you face difficult decisions or challenging circumstances. He will hear your requests, give you the ability to do what He asks, and then He will use that experience to build your faith. God truly is the Rewarder of those who diligently seek Him (Hebrews 11:6).

Now faith is the substance of things hoped for, the evidence of things not seen. . . .

By faith we understand that the worlds were framed by the word of God, so that the things which are seen were not made of things which are visible. . . .

Without faith it is impossible to please [God], for he who comes to God must believe that He is, and that He is a rewarder of those who diligently seek Him.

HEBREWS 11:1, 3, 6

God, who is rich in mercy, because of His great love with which He loved us, even when we were dead in trespasses, made us alive together with Christ (by grace you have been saved), and raised us up together, and made us sit together in the heavenly places in Christ Jesus.

EPHESIANS 2:4-6

I say, through the grace given to me, to everyone who is among you, not to think of himself more highly than he ought to think, but to think soberly, as God has dealt to each one a measure of faith.

ROMANS 12:3

Suddenly, a woman who had a flow of blood for twelve years came from behind and touched the hem of [Jesus'] garment. For she said to herself, "If only I may touch His garment, I shall be made well." But Jesus turned around, and when He saw her He said, "Be of good cheer, daughter; your faith has made you well." And the woman was made well from that hour.

MATTHEW 9:20–22

Faith comes by hearing, and hearing by the word of God.

ROMANS 10:17

For in [the gospel of Christ] the righteousness of God is revealed from faith to faith; as it is written, "The just shall live by faith."

ROMANS 1:17

You have been grieved by various trials, that the genuineness of your faith, being much more precious than gold that perishes, though it is tested by fire, may be found to praise, honor, and glory at the revelation of Jesus Christ, whom having not seen you love. Though now you do not see Him, yet believing, you rejoice with joy inexpressible and full of glory, receiving the end of your faith—the salvation of your souls.

1 PETER 1:6–9

THE FREEDOM THAT COMES WITH GOD'S FORGIVENESS

I f you are hurting, perhaps your pain is rooted in your struggle with sin, and the apostle Paul's words could be yours: "I want to do what is right, but I can't. I want to do what is good, but I don't" (Romans 7:18 NLT). Know that Jesus—by His victory over sin on the cross—offers you forgiveness (1 John 1:9). The Spirit does His transforming work to make you more like Jesus, so don't lose hope about changing your sinful ways. Forgiven for your sins and empowered by the Holy Spirit, you can live freely and boldly a life that points people to Jesus.

There is . . . now no condemnation to those who are in Christ Jesus, who do not walk according to the flesh, but according to the Spirit. For the law of the Spirit of life in Christ Jesus has made me free from the law of sin and death.

ROMANS 8:1–2

You, brethren, have been called to liberty; only do not use liberty as an opportunity for the flesh, but through love serve one another.

GALATIANS 5:13

"Whoever desires to save his life will lose it, but whoever loses his life for My sake will find it. For what profit is it to a man if he gains the whole world, and loses his own soul? Or what will a man give in exchange for his soul?"

MATTHEW 16:25–26

He who looks into the perfect law of liberty and continues in it, and is not a forgetful hearer but a doer of the work, this one will be blessed in what he does.

JAMES 1:25

Jesus said to those Jews who believed Him, "If you abide in My word, you are My disciples indeed. And you shall know the truth, and the truth shall make you free. . . .

If the Son makes you free, you shall be free indeed."

JOHN 8:32, 36

"Come to Me, all you who labor and are heavy laden, and I will give you rest. Take My yoke upon you and learn from Me, for I am gentle and lowly in heart, and you will find rest for your souls. For My yoke is easy and My burden is light."

MATTHEW 11:28–30

Stand fast therefore in the liberty by which Christ has made us free, and do not be entangled again with a yoke of bondage.

GALATIANS 5:1

All have sinned and fall short of the glory of God, being justified freely by His grace through the redemption that is in Christ Jesus.

ROMANS 3:23–24

THE IMPORTANCE OF OBEYING GOD

S ometimes we suffer pain because of a failure to obey God—either our own failure or someone else's. When you name Jesus as your Savior and make God the first priority in your life, you are saying that you will obey God and aim to please Him in all that you say and do. Such obedience clearly shows your love and respect for Him (John 14:21). And such obedience is the way to know God's joy and His pleasure in you.

Obeying God leads to a path of peace. Also, as it keeps sin from being a barrier between Him and you, your obedience enables you to live each moment in His blessed presence.

"If you love Me, keep My commandments. . . .

"He who has My commandments and keeps them, it is he who loves Me. And he who loves Me will be loved by My Father, and I will love him and manifest Myself to him."

JOHN 14:15, 21

"Behold, I set before you today a blessing and a curse: the blessing, if you obey the commandments of the LORD your God which I command you today; and the curse, if you do not obey the commandments of the LORD your God, but turn aside from the way which I command you today, to go after other gods which you have not known."

DEUTERONOMY 11:26–28

"This is what I commanded them, saying, 'Obey My voice, and I will be your God, and you shall be My people. And walk in all the ways that I have commanded you, that it may be well with you.'"

JEREMIAH 7:23

When [Jesus] had washed [His disciples'] feet, taken His garments, and sat down again, He said to them, "Do you know what I have done to you? You call Me Teacher and Lord, and you say well, for so I am. If I then, your Lord and Teacher, have washed your feet, you also ought to wash one another's feet. For I have given you an example, that you should do as I have done to you. Most assuredly, I say to you, a servant is not greater than his master; nor is he who is sent greater than he who sent him. If you know these things, blessed are you if you do them."

JOHN 13:12–17

*By this we know that we know Him, if we keep
His commandments. He who says, "I know
Him," and does not keep His commandments, is
a liar, and the truth is not in him. But whoever
keeps His word, truly the love of God is perfected
in him. By this we know that we are in Him. He
who says he abides in Him ought himself also to
walk just as He walked.*

1 JOHN 2:3–6

*"If you walk in My ways, to keep My statutes
and My commandments, as your father David
walked, then I will lengthen your days."*

1 KINGS 3:14

*Teach me to do Your will,
    For You are my God;
    Your Spirit is good.
    Lead me in the land of uprightness.*

PSALM 143:10

KEEPING YOUR EYES
ON JESUS

When you choose to live with Jesus as your Savior and Lord, you will know blessings beyond your imagining. Consider the blessing of being in relationship with the holy and almighty God of all creation. Then there is the blessing of being able to serve Him, a blessing that yields an abundance of joy and purpose. Followers of Jesus are also blessed by the gift of Jesus' Holy Spirit, the Comforter, the Teacher, the Guide, who is always with you. The world offers many distractions, loud voices, fleeting pleasures, and heartbreaking pain, but the Spirit will help you keep your eyes on Christ so that you can experience the richness of walking through life with Him and for Him.

Let us lay aside every weight, and the sin
which so easily ensnares us, and let us run with
endurance the race that is set before us, looking
unto Jesus, the author and finisher of our faith,
who for the joy that was set before Him endured
the cross, despising the shame, and has sat down
at the right hand of the throne of God.

HEBREWS 12:1–2

Whatever you do in word or deed, do all in the
name of the Lord Jesus, giving thanks to God the
Father through Him.

COLOSSIANS 3:17

I love those who love me,
    And those who seek me diligently will find me.

PROVERBS 8:17

*Seek the L*ORD *and His strength;*
     Seek His face evermore!
Remember His marvelous works which He has
          done,
     His wonders, and the judgments of His
          mouth.

1 CHRONICLES 16:11–12

*"You are My friends if you do whatever I
command you. No longer do I call you servants,
for a servant does not know what his master is
doing; but I have called you friends, for all things
that I heard from My Father I have made known
to you. You did not choose Me, but I chose you
and appointed you that you should go and bear
fruit, and that your fruit should remain, that
whatever you ask the Father in My name He may
give you."*

JOHN 15:14–16

In You, O Lord, I put my trust;
Let me never be put to shame. . . .
For You are my hope, O Lord GOD;
You are my trust from my youth. . . .
Let my mouth be filled with Your praise
And with Your glory all the day.

PSALM 71:1, 5, 8

Then [Jesus] said to [His twelve disciples], "If
anyone desires to come after Me, let him deny
himself, and take up his cross daily, and follow
Me. For whoever desires to save his life will lose
it, but whoever loses his life for My sake will save
it. For what profit is it to a man if he gains the
whole world, and is himself destroyed or lost?"

LUKE 9:23–25

SPIRITUAL HEALING

Being human means stumbling spiritually; it means sinning even when you don't want to sin. But you don't need to stay stuck in that guilty and sinful state. Instead, go to God to receive His forgiveness. He wants to welcome you back into close fellowship with Him. You who have named Jesus as your Lord have in Him a Savior who is willing to pick you up, forgive your sin, and cleanse you from that unrighteousness (1 John 1:9). The Lord is good, He is ready to forgive, and His mercy is abundant to all the guilty who call on Him. So never hesitate to turn to your holy God. Humbly confess your sin, receive His forgiveness, and enjoy a restored relationship with Him.

You, Lord, are good, and ready to forgive,
    And abundant in mercy to all those who call
        upon You.
Give ear, O LORD, to my prayer;
    And attend to the voice of my supplications.
In the day of my trouble I will call upon You,
    For You will answer me.

                                PSALM 86:5–7

One thing I do, forgetting those things which
are behind and reaching forward to those things
which are ahead, I press toward the goal for the
prize of the upward call of God in Christ Jesus.

                        PHILIPPIANS 3:13–14

He who covers his sins will not prosper,
    But whoever confesses and forsakes them will
        have mercy.

                            PROVERBS 28:13

Have you not known?

Have you not heard?

The everlasting God, the LORD,

The Creator of the ends of the earth,

Neither faints nor is weary.

His understanding is unsearchable.

He gives power to the weak,

And to those who have no might He increases

strength. . . .

Those who wait on the LORD

Shall renew their strength;

They shall mount up with wings like eagles,

They shall run and not be weary,

They shall walk and not faint.

ISAIAH 40:28–29, 31

"I will seek what was lost and bring back what was driven away, bind up the broken and strengthen what was sick; but I will destroy the fat and the strong, and feed them in judgment. . . . Thus they shall know that I, the LORD their God, am with them, and they, the house of Israel, are My people," says the Lord GOD.

"You are My flock, the flock of My pasture; you are men, and I am your God," says the Lord GOD.

EZEKIEL 34:16, 30–31

HAVING AN EFFECTIVE
PRAYER LIFE

Whatever the source of your pain, be open and honest with your heavenly Father about it. After all, having an ongoing honest conversation with God throughout your day is a blessed privilege of a Christian's life. In prayer, you can draw close to the One who loves you unconditionally, and you receive from Him all the comfort and encouragement you need. He will listen to your prayers and answer them. He will respond wisely and lovingly, for your good and in His perfect timing. And He will gladly walk through life with you and talk with you each step of the way as your Guide, Counselor, Protector, Provider, Shepherd, and Friend.

*Be anxious for nothing, but in everything by prayer
and supplication, with thanksgiving, let your
requests be made known to God; and the peace of
God, which surpasses all understanding, will guard
your hearts and minds through Christ Jesus.*

PHILIPPIANS 4:6–7

Give ear, O LORD, *to my prayer;*
        And attend to the voice of my supplications.
In the day of my trouble I will call upon You,
        For You will answer me.

PSALM 86:6–7

*"Assuredly, I say to you, whatever you bind on
earth will be bound in heaven, and whatever you
loose on earth will be loosed in heaven.*

*"Again I say to you that if two of you agree
on earth concerning anything that they ask, it
will be done for them by My Father in heaven."*

MATTHEW 18:18–19

Let us therefore come boldly to the throne of grace, that we may obtain mercy and find grace to help in time of need.

HEBREWS 4:16

Take up the whole armor of God, that you may be able to withstand in the evil day, and having done all, to stand.

Stand therefore, having girded your waist with truth, having put on the breastplate of righteousness, and having shod your feet with the preparation of the gospel of peace; above all, taking the shield of faith with which you will be able to quench all the fiery darts of the wicked one. And take the helmet of salvation, and the sword of the Spirit, which is the word of God; praying always with all prayer and supplication in the Spirit, being watchful to this end with all perseverance and supplication for all the saints.

EPHESIANS 6:13–18

The effective, fervent prayer of a righteous man avails much.

JAMES 5:16

"So I say to you, ask, and it will be given to you; seek, and you will find; knock, and it will be opened to you."

LUKE 11:9

"When you pray, you shall not be like the hypocrites. For they love to pray standing in the synagogues and on the corners of the streets, that they may be seen by men. Assuredly, I say to you, they have their reward. But you, when you pray, go into your room, and when you have shut your door, pray to your Father who is in the secret place; and your Father who sees in secret will reward you openly."

MATTHEW 6:5–6

TRUTH FROM THE BIBLE ABOUT . . .

THE SUFFICIENCY OF JESUS

Fifteen hundred years ago Saint Augustine commented on the fact that within every human heart is "a God-shaped hole." That hole exists because nothing and no one except Jesus Himself will satisfy your desire for love, your quest for purpose, your hope for fulfillment. When you realize this truth—when you consider that a God-shaped hole in your heart may be contributing to the pain you're dealing with today—life becomes simpler: your focus is the Lord. When you open your heart and your life to the Lord, He empowers you to live each moment for Him. As you walk through each day with Jesus, you will see Him provide all you need.

*God is able to make all grace abound toward you,
that you, always having all sufficiency in all things,
may have an abundance for every good work.*

2 CORINTHIANS 9:8

*Jesus said to [the people], "I am the bread of life.
He who comes to Me shall never hunger, and he
who believes in Me shall never thirst."*

JOHN 6:35

*Let your conduct be without covetousness; be
content with such things as you have. For He
Himself has said, "I will never leave you nor
forsake you." So we may boldly say:*

    "The LORD is my helper;
    I will not fear.
    What can man do to me?" . . .
  *Jesus Christ is the same yesterday, today,
and forever.*

HEBREWS 13:5–6, 8

*Seeing then that we have a great High Priest
who has passed through the heavens, Jesus the
Son of God, let us hold fast our confession.
For we do not have a High Priest who cannot
sympathize with our weaknesses, but was in all
points tempted as we are, yet without sin. Let us
therefore come boldly to the throne of grace, that
we may obtain mercy and find grace to help in
time of need.*

Hebrews 4:14–16

*[Jesus] said to [Paul], "My grace is sufficient
for you, for My strength is made perfect in
weakness." Therefore most gladly I will rather
boast in my infirmities, that the power of Christ
may rest upon me.*

2 Corinthians 12:9

*In [Jesus] dwells all the fullness of the Godhead
bodily; and you are complete in Him, who is the
head of all principality and power.*

Colossians 2:9–10

[The resurrected] Jesus came and spoke to [the eleven disciples], saying, "All authority has been given to Me in heaven and on earth. Go therefore and make disciples of all the nations, baptizing them in the name of the Father and of the Son and of the Holy Spirit, teaching them to observe all things that I have commanded you; and lo, I am with you always, even to the end of the age." Amen.

MATTHEW 28:18–20

I can do all things through Christ who strengthens me.

PHILIPPIANS 4:13

My help comes from the LORD,
*   Who made heaven and earth.*
He will not allow your foot to be moved;
*   He who keeps you will not slumber.*

PSALM 121:2–3

TRUTH FROM THE BIBLE ABOUT . . .
THE GRACE OF GOD

Whatever prompted the hurt you've experienced, know that God's grace can bring peace, hope, and healing. Grace has been defined as "undeserved favor," and God's grace is adequate for anything and everything that you experience in this life. One beautiful thing about grace is that God does not withdraw His grace when you stumble and fall. Instead, acting with grace, He gently picks you up and enables you to take the next step. You can always find at His throne of grace whatever help you need whenever you need it. You can run to the Lord in times of trouble, when your heart is breaking, at life's crossroads, and during the darkest of nights. He is waiting for you with open arms.

The LORD God is a sun and shield;
* The LORD will give grace and glory;*
* No good thing will He withhold*
* From those who walk uprightly.*
O LORD of hosts,
* Blessed is the man who trusts in You!*

PSALM 84:11–12

He who raised up the Lord Jesus will also raise
us up with Jesus, and will present us with you.
For all things are for your sakes, that grace,
having spread through the many, may cause
thanksgiving to abound to the glory of God.

2 CORINTHIANS 4:14–15

He who loves purity of heart
* And has grace on his lips,*
* The king will be his friend.*

PROVERBS 22:11

Blessed be the God and Father of our Lord Jesus Christ, who has blessed us with every spiritual blessing in the heavenly places in Christ, just as He chose us in Him before the foundation of the world, that we should be holy and without blame before Him in love, having predestined us to adoption as sons by Jesus Christ to Himself, according to the good pleasure of His will, to the praise of the glory of His grace, by which He made us accepted in the Beloved.

EPHESIANS 1:3–6

All have sinned and fall short of the glory of God, being justified freely by His grace through the redemption that is in Christ Jesus, whom God set forth as a propitiation by His blood, through faith, to demonstrate His righteousness, because in His forbearance God had passed over the sins that were previously committed, to demonstrate at the present time His righteousness, that He might be just and the justifier of the one who has faith in Jesus.

ROMANS 3:23–26

By grace you have been saved through faith, and
that not of yourselves; it is the gift of God, not of
works, lest anyone should boast.

Ephesians 2:8–9

The law was given through Moses, but grace and
truth came through Jesus Christ.

John 1:17

The free gift [of forgiveness and eternal life]
is not like the offense. For if by the one man's
offense many died, much more the grace of God
and the gift by the grace of the one Man, Jesus
Christ, abounded to many. . . . For if by the one
man's offense death reigned through the one,
much more those who receive abundance of grace
and of the gift of righteousness will reign in life
through the One, Jesus Christ.

Romans 5:15, 17

THE LOVE OF GOD

Life's hard times—combined with whispers from the enemy—may make you doubt God's love for you. In moments like that, keep your eyes fixed on the cross: Jesus gave His life so that you might know the forgiveness of your sin and life eternal with Him. The love evident on the cross is indescribable, immeasurable, and completely unshakable: "Neither death nor life, nor angels nor principalities nor powers, nor things present nor things to come, nor height nor depth, nor any other created thing, shall be able to separate us from the love of God which is in Christ Jesus our Lord" (Romans 8:38–39). This is a promise to you. And God the Promise Maker is God the Promise Keeper.

For God so loved the world that He gave His
only begotten Son, that whoever believes in Him
should not perish but have everlasting life.

JOHN 3:16

Behold what manner of love the Father has
bestowed on us, that we should be called children
of God!

1 JOHN 3:1

In this is love, not that we loved God, but that He
loved us and sent His Son to be the propitiation
for our sins. Beloved, if God so loved us, we also
ought to love one another.

No one has seen God at any time. If we love
one another, God abides in us, and His love has
been perfected in us.

1 JOHN 4:10–12

Take careful heed to do the commandment and the law which Moses the servant of the LORD commanded you, to love the LORD your God, to walk in all His ways, to keep His commandments, to hold fast to Him, and to serve Him with all your heart and with all your soul.

JOSHUA 22:5

"As the Father loved Me, I also have loved you; abide in My love. If you keep My commandments, you will abide in My love, just as I have kept My Father's commandments and abide in His love."

JOHN 15:9–10

The LORD has appeared of old to me, saying:
    "Yes, I have loved you with an
        everlasting love;
    Therefore with lovingkindness I have
        drawn you."

JEREMIAH 31:3

I am persuaded that neither death nor life,
nor angels nor principalities nor powers, nor
things present nor things to come, nor height nor
depth, nor any other created thing, shall be able
to separate us from the love of God which is in
Christ Jesus our Lord.

ROMANS 8:38–39

"A new commandment I give to you, that you
love one another; as I have loved you, that you
also love one another. By this all will know that
you are My disciples, if you have love for one
another."

JOHN 13:34–35

Beloved, let us love one another, for love is of
God; and everyone who loves is born of God and
knows God. He who does not love does not know
God, for God is love.

1 JOHN 4:7–8

TRUTH

that God's love for you . . .

TRUTH THAT GOD'S LOVE FOR YOU . . .
BRINGS HEALING

It makes total sense that the God who created you can also heal you physically, mentally, emotionally, spiritually: your Creator God is your Great Physician as well. Thank God for His healing power, and don't hesitate to ask Him for His healing touch whenever you are hurting. Whatever the source and whatever the site of your pain, whether you are physically ill, brokenhearted by a relationship, or overwhelmed by the demands of life, you can experience the Lord as your great Comforter. He is Jehovah-jireh, the great and mighty Healer, and He is waiting with open arms for you to come to Him.

"To you who fear My name
  The Sun of Righteousness shall arise
  With healing in His wings."

MALACHI 4:2

O LORD my God, I cried out to You,
  And You healed me.
O LORD, You brought my soul up from the grave;
  You have kept me alive.

PSALM 30:2–3

[The LORD] heals the brokenhearted
  And binds up their wounds.
He counts the number of the stars;
  He calls them all by name.
Great is our Lord, and mighty in power;
  His understanding is infinite.
The LORD lifts up the humble;
  He casts the wicked down to the ground.

PSALM 147:3–6

"The Spirit of the Lord GOD is upon Me,
   Because the LORD has anointed Me…
   To comfort all who mourn,
To console those who mourn in Zion,
   To give them beauty for ashes,
   The oil of joy for mourning,
   The garment of praise for the spirit of
      heaviness;
   That they may be called trees of
      righteousness,
   The planting of the LORD, that He may be
      glorified."

ISAIAH 61:1–3

Then great multitudes came to [Jesus], having
with them the lame, blind, mute, maimed, and
many others; and they laid them down at Jesus'
feet, and He healed them.

MATTHEW 15:30

Is anyone among you sick? Let him call for the elders of the church, and let them pray over him, anointing him with oil in the name of the Lord. And the prayer of faith will save the sick, and the Lord will raise him up. And if he has committed sins, he will be forgiven. Confess your trespasses to one another, and pray for one another, that you may be healed. The effective, fervent prayer of a righteous man avails much.

JAMES 5:14–16

"The Spirit of the LORD is upon Me,
Because He has anointed Me
To preach the gospel to the poor;
He has sent Me to heal the brokenhearted,
To proclaim liberty to the captives
And recovery of sight to the blind,
To set at liberty those who are oppressed;
To proclaim the acceptable year of the LORD."

LUKE 4:18–19

TRUTH THAT GOD'S LOVE FOR YOU . . .
IS YOUR ETERNAL INHERITANCE

P ain can function like blinders: you can't see or even imagine anything beyond that moment. But as God's child, you can be sure that He has planned a glorious eternal future for you: He has provided a way for you to live in His presence forever. And that eternal life spent in the presence of the God of love is "an inheritance incorruptible and undefiled . . . that does not fade away" (1 Peter 1:4). God has promised you who name Jesus as your Savior and Lord the hope of heaven, and no person, no event, no thing can take it away. Rest in the Lord as you keep your eyes on Him. Live each moment for Him, faithfully serve your risen Savior, and be confident about your eternal future.

The Lord knows the days of the upright,
*   And their inheritance shall be forever.*

PSALM 37:18

Blessed be the God and Father of our Lord Jesus
Christ, who according to His abundant mercy
has begotten us again to a living hope through the
resurrection of Jesus Christ from the dead, to an
inheritance incorruptible and undefiled and that
does not fade away, reserved in heaven for you,
who are kept by the power of God through faith
for salvation ready to be revealed in the last time.

1 PETER 1:3–5

Having been set free from sin, and having
become slaves of God, you have your fruit to
holiness, and the end, everlasting life. For the
wages of sin is death, but the gift of God is eternal
life in Christ Jesus our Lord.

ROMANS 6:22–23

May the God of all grace, who called us to
His eternal glory by Christ Jesus, after you have
suffered a while, perfect, establish, strengthen,
and settle you.

1 PETER 5:10

"Whoever eats My flesh and drinks My blood
has eternal life, and I will raise him up at the last
day. For My flesh is food indeed, and My blood is
drink indeed."

JOHN 6:54–55

We know that if our earthly house, this tent, is
destroyed, we have a building from God, a house
not made with hands, eternal in the heavens.

2 CORINTHIANS 5:1

Having been justified by His grace we should
become heirs according to the hope of eternal life.

TITUS 3:7

[God] has delivered [those of us He has saved]
from the power of darkness and conveyed us into
the kingdom of the Son of His love, in whom
we have redemption through His blood, the
forgiveness of sins.

He is the image of the invisible God, the
firstborn over all creation. For by Him all things
were created that are in heaven and that are on
earth, visible and invisible, whether thrones or
dominions or principalities or powers. All things
were created through Him and for Him.

COLOSSIANS 1:13–16

TRUTH THAT GOD'S LOVE FOR YOU . . .
WILL NEVER CHANGE

Often the hurt we feel in life results from an unexpected incident, an unanticipated turn of events, an unwanted change. And sometimes it's the result of a poor decision we've made that brings on shame and even doubt about God's love for us. In these stormy waters of life, though, cling to the lifeline truth that His love for you will not diminish—no matter what. He has loved you since He knit you together in your mother's womb, and He will love you for eternity. Nothing you do will ever make Him love you less. The God of the universe—who numbers the hair on your head—is invested in His relationship with you. And His immeasurable love for you will never change.

*I am persuaded that neither death nor life,
nor angels nor principalities nor powers, nor
things present nor things to come, nor height nor
depth, nor any other created thing, shall be able
to separate us from the love of God which is in
Christ Jesus our Lord.*

Romans 8:38–39

*"I know the thoughts that I think toward you,
says the Lord, thoughts of peace and not of evil,
to give you a future and a hope. Then you will
call upon Me and go and pray to Me, and I will
listen to you. And you will seek Me and find Me,
when you search for Me with all your heart."*

Jeremiah 29:11–13

*"God did not send his Son into the world to
condemn the world, but to save the world
through him."*

John 3:17

"I am the vine, you are the branches. He who abides in Me, and I in him, bears much fruit; for without Me you can do nothing. If anyone does not abide in Me, he is cast out as a branch and is withered; and they gather them and throw them into the fire, and they are burned. If you abide in Me, and My words abide in you, you will ask what you desire, and it shall be done for you. . . . As the Father loved Me, I also have loved you; abide in My love."

JOHN 15:5–7, 9

The love of Christ compels us, because we judge thus: that if One died for all, then all died; and He died for all, that those who live should live no longer for themselves, but for Him who died for them and rose again. . . . If anyone is in Christ, he is a new creation; old things have passed away; behold, all things have become new.

2 CORINTHIANS 5:14–15, 17

He who sows sparingly will also reap sparingly, and he who sows bountifully will also reap bountifully. So let each one give as he purposes in his heart, not grudgingly or of necessity; for God loves a cheerful giver. And God is able to make all grace abound toward you, that you, always having all sufficiency in all things, may have an abundance for every good work.

2 CORINTHIANS 9:6–8

My God shall supply all your need according to His riches in glory by Christ Jesus.

PHILIPPIANS 4:19

God is light and in Him is no darkness at all. If we say that we have fellowship with Him, and walk in darkness, we lie and do not practice the truth. But if we walk in the light as He is in the light, we have fellowship with one another, and the blood of Jesus Christ His Son cleanses us from all sin.

1 JOHN 1:5–7

NURTURES HOPE FOR NOW
AND FOR ETERNITY

Pain can bring hopelessness as the enemy relentlessly attempts to wear down God's children. But your loving heavenly Father holds out to you—without hesitation and without any fine-print disclaimers—the wonderful hope of His good plans for you, hope that is rooted in His amazing love for you. Your relationship with your heavenly Father—a relationship that you will work on building and strengthening for the rest of your life—is a place where you can be known and loved. And your confidence in God's love for you will nurture your hope in Him—hope for this life as well as for life eternal.

*Through the L*ORD*'s mercies we are not consumed,*
    Because His compassions fail not.
They are new every morning;
    Great is Your faithfulness.
"The Lord is my portion," says my soul,
    "Therefore I hope in Him!"

LAMENTATIONS 3:22–24

*"Blessed is the man who trusts in the L*ORD*,*
    *And whose hope is the L*ORD*.*
For he shall be like a tree planted by the waters,
    Which spreads out its roots by the river,
    And will not fear when heat comes;
    But its leaf will be green,
    And will not be anxious in the year of
        drought,
    Nor will cease from yielding fruit."

JEREMIAH 17:7–8

The LORD is good to those who wait for Him,
    To the soul who seeks Him.
It is good that one should hope and wait quietly
    For the salvation of the LORD.

                    LAMENTATIONS 3:25–26

May the God of hope fill you with all joy and
peace in believing, that you may abound
in hope by the power of the Holy Spirit.

                    ROMANS 15:13

Having been justified by faith, we have peace
with God through our Lord Jesus Christ, through
whom also we have access by faith into this grace
in which we stand, and rejoice in hope of the glory
of God. And not only that, but we also glory in
tribulations, knowing that tribulation produces
perseverance; and perseverance, character; and
character, hope. Now hope does not disappoint,
because the love of God has been poured out in our
hearts by the Holy Spirit who was given to us.

                    ROMANS 5:1–5

My soul, wait silently for God alone,
    For my expectation is from Him.
He only is my rock and my salvation;
    He is my defense;
    I shall not be moved.
In God is my salvation and my glory;
    The rock of my strength,
    And my refuge, is in God.

PSALM 62:5–7

You are my hiding place and my shield;
    I hope in Your word. . . .
Uphold me according to Your word, that I may live;
    And do not let me be ashamed of my hope.
Hold me up, and I shall be safe,
    And I shall observe Your statutes continually.

PSALM 119:114, 116–117